CARAVAGGIO – DIARIES

(Extracts from Fr. Marius Zerafa's Diaries)

Transcribed and edited by Catherine Sinclair Galea

First published in Malta 2004 by:

© Grimand Co Ltd 2004
grimand@medzone.com.mt

In association with:

Design: Box Design
Prepress and Printing: Gutenburg Press Ltd
Editing: Catherine Sinclair Galea
Proof reading: Debbie Jackson

Photographs courtesy of Fr. M.J.Zerafa except:
Mark Scicluna - Cover Photo
Tony Mangion – pgs 166 and back cover flap
Curia Archives – pg 12, 143
Jovan Mizzi – pg 129
Brigadier Maurice Calleja – pgs 86, 87
Malta Tourism Authority – pg 24

Newspaper cuttings courtesy of:
The Times – pgs xi, 14, 18, 92, 98, 103, 110, 135, 136, 137, 140, 162, 164, 167,168
The Sunday Times – pgs 3, 90
L-Orizzont – pgs 16, 105
Media.link – pgs 105, 163
Standard Publications Ltd., publishers of The Malta Independent – pgs 15, 112, 137

ISBN: 99932-0-322-X

Editor's Note

It has been a pleasure to work on The Caravaggio Diaries. To many, Father Marius Zerafa is not very different from a work of art. His presence and company is much sought after and appreciated, he has frequently been referred to as one of our national treasures. Fr. Marius could have become an international lost treasure had the protagonists of the Caravaggio theft succeeded in what would have been Malta's first case of kidnapping. Although Father Zerafa's Dominican Prior joked that he would have paid the thieves to keep him, Father Marius managed to salvage the painting as well as emerge, none the worse for wear, from a rather trying situation.

While Fr. Marius Zerafa attributes the successful recovery of the St. Jerome painting to '...the Divinity that shapes our ends, rough hew them as we may...' few are aware of the personal cost and challenges faced by a Dominican priest turned sleuth, whilst carrying out his various duties as Director of Museums. This is also the reason for including events that might otherwise seem unrelated.

While this story merits a written record in its own right, the editor has found little to alter in the way of sharp prose and wit that presents a factual diary. Sometimes full sentences in specific tenses not normally used in diary format, as well as intervening notes, have had to be inserted for clarity.

The diary, accompanying photos and press cuttings offer a kaleidoscope of events and anecdotes that provide a colourful text to the Maltese, as well as to the International reader.

The diary excerpts reproduced here, are from diary entries that comprise fifty full years and will, one day, be published in full.

C.S.G.

May 2004

Dedicated to the memory of a young man who unfortunately did not survive this *strange eventful episode.*

"Neguzjanti tad-droga bagħtu fjuri u ġew għall-funeral"
"Lil ħija mhux se nġibuh lura, iżda ejja nippruvaw insalvaw lil tfal u żgħażagħ oħra."
Il-Ħelsien – 25/06/1993

"Drug dealers sent flowers and attended the funeral"
"We will never be able to bring my brother back, but let us try to save other children and teenagers."
Il-Ħelsien – 25/06/1993

CARAVAGGIO - DIARIES

Contents

Chapter 1
St Jerome goes into the wilderness 1

Chapter 2
Pictor Celeberrimus 5

Chapter 3
Ministers & Monsignori 13

Chapter 4
Merisi 23

Chapter 5
Projects & Plans 45

Chapter 6
Day of providence 83

Chapter 7
Twisted by knaves to make a trap for fools 97

Chapter 8
Brought back on a golden platter 167

Lecturing at the Smithsonian

CARAVAGGIO - DIARIES

Biography

FR. MARIUS J. ZERAFA

O.P., S.Th.L. & Lic., Dr.Sc.Soc., B.A. Hons. (Lond),
A.R.Hist.S. (Lond)

Born in Vittoriosa, 13th October 1929, son of
Joseph Zerafa M.B.E. and Maria nè Boffa,
nephew of Sir Paul Boffa Kt., O.B.E., M.D.,
Prime Minister of Malta.

Father Marius joined the Dominican Order at the age of sixteen. Soon after
that, he was sent to England and furthered his studies at 'Blackfriars' in
Oxford, (1945-52). He then went to Rome (1952–54) where he obtained
the S.Th.B. and Dip. Sc.Soc. He returned to Rome for another two years
(1960-62) gaining his Lectorate ad Licentiate in Sacred Theology and a
doctorate in Social Sciences. Later he was awarded a Diploma in Art
History from the Rome State University and a BA (Hons) degree in Art
History from the University of London.

He has followed courses at the Sorbonne and at the Ecole de Louvre,
Paris (1963 and 1966); at the University of Florence (1965 and 1968); at
the Brera, Milan, and at the Fondazione Cini, Venice (1965). He is a
member of the Accademia Tiberina, Rome has been awarded the French
decoration "Chevalier dans l'Ordre des Arts et des Lettres' and is also an
Associate of the Royal Historical Society, London.

Fr. Zerafa joined the Museums Department in 1970 as Assistant

Fr. Zerafa in his studio

Fr. Zerafa with his full size copy of 'Angelico's Annunciation'

CARAVAGGIO - DIARIES

Curator of Fine Arts and was responsible for the setting up of Malta's National Museum of Fine Arts, Valletta, later becoming Director of Museums in Malta and Gozo. It was during this period that he was involved in the recovery of the painting, St. Jerome, by Caravaggio.

Fr. Zerafa has been invited to lecture at the Smithsonian, Washington; at Fordham University, New York; at the Dominican Curia Generalizia, Rome; at Aspen Museum, Colorado; at Budapest Museum; and has helped organize art exhibitions in America, Britain, Russia and other European countries.

He was Chairman of Government and other Committees and is still Chairman of the Archdiocesan Commission for Sacred Art. He is also a member of the Cultural Patrimony Commission and is chaplain to the Third Age University and the British Legion.

Fr. Zerafa retired from the Museums Department though he continues to lecture at the University of Malta, the Alliance Française and

'Sometimes I behaved...'

other cultural centres. He has taught at various schools and colleges and is at present Professor of Sacred Art at the University of St. Thomas, Rome.

Father has carried out restoration on work by Mattia Preti, Favray and other Masters. His own paintings and sculptures are to be found in collections in Malta and abroad.

His writing includes articles on Social Doctrine and Art History and contributions to Art Encyclopaedias.

The Arts, reading and travelling are listed as some of Fr. Marius' favourite recreations and he is known to be happiest in the company of faithful friends and students whether on study tours, lectures or informal meetings at the cafés outside his priory. It was Fr.'s invaluable advice while working on Caravaggio.com and with the Caravaggio foundation that inspired the final publication of this story of the theft and recovery of the Caravaggio paintings.

STOLEN CARAVAGGIO

Sir, – Sometime ago I was irked by Fr. Marius Zerafa's comment "one day the whole story will come out" in his letter entitled "Stolen Caravaggio" (May 18).

Now I am all the more irked that neither Fr. Zerafa nor the Minister of Education and the Interior, nor for that matter the Director of Information ever bothered to enlighten an "intelligent" public as to the true facts about the stolen Caravaggio.

Given the circumstances I feel it would be most correct to demand an explanation from either Fr. Zerafa, or the Minister of Education, or, for that matter, the Director of Information.

Shall I stand to be entertained to be deluded once again by a conspicuous absence of a reply? I sincerely hope not!

Yours truly,
"STORY TELLER",
Sliema.

The Times - Tuesday, July 10, 1991

STQARRIJA FIL-PARLAMENT DWAR IS-SEJBIEN
TAL-PITTURA TAL-CARAVAGGIO

ONOR. EDWARD FENECH ADAMI - Prim Ministru

"Nixtieq nirringrazzja, b'mod partikolari, lid-Direttur tal-Muzewijiet Patri Marius Zerafa (Onor. Membri: Hear, hear) ghall-interess li ha u ghall-pacenzja kbira li mexa biha, il-prudenza u s-sehem shih li kellu biex illum l-investigazzjonijiet taw dan ir-rizultat posittiv..."

STATEMENT IN PARIAMENT ON THE RECOVERY OF CARAVAGGIO'S PAINTING
HON. EDWARD FENECH ADAMI - Prime Minister

I would particularly like to thank the Director of Museums, Fr Marius Zerafa (Hon. Members: hear, hear), for his patience, interest and the competent manner in which he pursued this matter greatly contributing to this positive result.

Chapter 1

ST JEROME GOES INTO THE WILDERNESS

Thursday, 27th

The year 1984 is drawing to a close. After 25 happy years at the Dominican Priory in Valletta, I have just moved to the Jesus of Nazareth Priory in Sliema. It has not been an easy passage, but I have fought 'the good fight', things have run their course, my faith has kept me. Tonight I will sleep in my new room - still in a mess - but enjoying a lovely view over Marsamxett Harbour.

Saturday, 29th

Finished painting my new room this morning and then went to Valletta where I was awarded a trophy 'Artist of the Year' by the Art Association 'Nghinu bl'Arti'. A wet dreary day. The Minister who had to preside arrived late – as usual.

View over Marsamxett Harbour

After the presentation, I came back home hoping to have a good rest. This was not to be. At about 7 pm I received an urgent phone call from Mrs. Cutajar, [wife of Dominic, curator of the Museum of St. John's Co Cathedral]. She was obviously shaken – something terrible had happened – too terrible, it seemed, to repeat over the phone. The Cutajars live close to the Priory. I asked them to come over at once. Dominic was in very bad shape – all he could utter was "Hadulna l-Caravaggio" (they have taken 'our' Caravaggio). I was afraid he would collapse. Somehow, I managed to calm him down. In broken sentences he told me what had happened. A tourist had come to the Museum to see the 'St. Jerome' but a chain stretched across the entrance to the room, with a label 'WORK IN PROGRESS', had barred her way. She went to Dominic's office to complain. Dominic knew very well that no work was going on at that time. As he went into the room where the painting was meant to be, he got the shock of his life.

The heavy frame had been lowered from its place on the wall and was lying on the floor. The

Caravaggio masterpiece stolen from St. John's Museum

by a Staff Reporter

ONE of Malta's priceless art treasures — Caravaggio's "St. Jerome" — was stolen from the St. John's Co-Cathedral Museum in Valetta yesterday afternoon in a daring robbery which stunned Maltese and foreign art lovers.

"St. Jerome", painted by Michelangelo Merisi da Caravaggio (1573-1610) for the Chapel of St. Catherine of the Langue of Italy in St. John's, is one of two priceless Caravaggios in Malta, the other being of course the famous *Beheading of St. John* which hangs in the Oratory of St. John's.

The theft must have occurred between 3 p.m. and 5 p.m., when the Museum was about to be closed for the day. The thieves probably entered the way visitors normally do, quietly removed the painting from its frame, and then lowered it from the window close by onto St. John's Square, where one or more accomplices must have been waiting. No other items were reported stolen. The Museum authorities found the window open, which lends credence to this probable sequence of events.

The duty magistrate carried out an inquiry while Police made their investigations.

The painting which measures 117cm by 157 cm, shows St. Jerome, naked to the waist, sitting up on his couch and writing. (He was the translator of the Bible into Latin.) It is possible that Grand Master Alof de Wignacourt (who had commissioned a portrait from Caravag-

gio, which now hangs in the Louvre, Paris) was the model for St. Jerome.

In the bottom right corner of the picture can be seen the coat of arms of Fra Ippolito Malaspina, Prior of Naples, who may have helped Caravaggio to come to Malta in 1608.

The painting was restored in 1956 at the *Istituto Centrale del Restauro* in Rome.

* * *

The theft of "St. Jerome" is the most spectacular of a series of art thefts in Malta in the last few months.

A 16th century painting of Our Lady of Divine Providence, by Sicilian artist Giuseppe Vel-

asco, was one of a number of paintings stolen from a wayside chapel in Siggiewi on the night of July 28-29. Velasco's work was the titular painting of the chapel dedicated to Our Lady of Divine Providence situated close to the residential homes for the handicapped. The frame was left behind.

In September, a priceless 306-year-old painting by Mattia Preti was stolen from the old Chapel of St. Matthew at Tal-Maqluba, limits of Qrendi. The painting, showing the killing of St. Matthew while he celebrated Mass, was discovered missing on September 19. The frame of the painting was also left behind.

The Sunday Times - December 30, 1984

canvas had been cut away from its stretcher. The painting was nowhere to be seen.

The tourist was visiting St. John's Museum on the last Saturday of 1984. As normally happens at this time of year, almost all of the guides were taking up their annual leave. On this day, only one custodian was available - and he was downstairs at the desk. The thieves, evidently aware of this situation, took advantage of it, and made off with the painting.

This was the beginning of a seemingly unending saga, seriously punctuated with episodes of worry, agony and anger.

MICHEL-ANGE DE CARAVAGE.

Chapter 2

PICTOR CELEBERRIMUS

Caravaggio, or to give him his full name, Michelangelo Merisi da Caravaggio, hardly needs an introduction. In his own lifetime, he was referred to as *pictor celeberrimus* or *pictor egregius*. He had led an exciting life and his wild escapades had eventually led him to Malta where he had been received as a Knight. The Order of St. John wished to honour him 'as Apelles had been honoured in Greece'.

While on the Island, he painted two portraits of Grandmaster Alof de Wignacourt, a 'Sleeping Cupid', other portraits and sacred subjects including works that are in foreign museums or that are considered lost.

In Malta we are fortunate to have his masterpiece '*The Beheading of St. John*' which he painted during his first year in the Order. It is the only painting he ever signed - f Michelang... –'f' denoting 'fra', (brother) probably to demonstrate that he had made it as a Knight of Malta.

An old engraving showing the de-frocking of a knight in the oratory of St. John's Co-Cathedral

This work of art adorned the Oratory of St. John's Co Cathedral where Caravaggio had also been received into the Order. It would have served to remind the young knights that they were likely to die in defence of their faith. The defence of the Island against the Islamic Turks was one mission particularly assigned to the Christian Knights. (One of the figures in the group around the martyred St. John, the 'jailer' with a bunch of keys in his belt, has been described as being dressed as a Turk.) Later on, the painting would look down on the assembly of Knights gathered to expel this *pictor egregius*, 'tamquam membrum foetidum et putridum' (like a fetid and putrid limb) who had left the Island without permission after being imprisoned for yet another crime.

In the '*Beheading...*', Caravaggio not only showed his particular technique - painting 'alla prima' (without preparatory drawings), on a canvas prepared in red and glazed in black - but also gave a most superb example of his, then novel, use of light. He employs this 'luce di cantina' effect (a source of light entering a dark room or cellar spotlighting the subject) to model his figures, compose his groups and give a sense of drama to the violent action taking place before our eyes. Quite often this lighting effect is illustrative of the light of grace.

Caravaggio's monumental figures go about their given tasks while an old woman expresses horror at the drama taking place on stage. All action focuses on the figure of St. John - a victim (wearing the sacrificial lambskin) that Caravaggio could have identified with. The artist himself was under sentence of death. This too may, perhaps, explain why he signed his name in the blood oozing out of the neck of the saint.

The 'Beheading of St. John', was described as the 'quadro del secolo' when it was restored in Rome in the 1950's.

This great masterpiece can now be seen in its true splendour after its recent restoration in Florence in the late 1990's.

'The Beheading...' has tended to overshadow yet another Caravaggio masterpiece – a smaller painting – the 'St. Jerome'. This is a beautiful pyramidal composition and a brilliant exercise in the study of light and in the fine rendering of the features of the saint. It is also a magnificent study of old age, meditation and sanctity. An old man is seated at a table that is cleverly used by the artist to create depth in the picture. A still life - a crucifix, candlestick, skull and stone completes the scene. Light falls upon an open book and a weathered hand draws one's attention up to a beautifully-modelled head. It was probably painted for a Knight and must have belonged to Ippolito Malaspina whose crest was inserted at the lower right hand corner of the painting. The Knight Malaspina presented the 'St. Jerome', together with a number of other paintings, to St. John's Co-Cathedral.

The painting of 'St. Jerome' was hung in the Chapel of Italy within St. John's Co-Cathedral. It is probable that it was raised to a position above the passageway when Preti carried out structural alterations in the Cathedral.

The painting of 'St. Jerome', had remained in the chapel of Italy for years until the St. John's Museum was inaugurated - a worthy monument to its founder - Mgr Edward Coleiro. Mgr. Coleiro was a very good friend with whom I worked for many years – ever since we organised the cultural lectures at the Catholic Institute and held the first Biennale of Sacred Arts in St. John's that has been such a success. We often disagreed but I always had the highest respect for his honesty and for his energy.

Unfortunately a foreign expert had decided that the '*St. Jerome*' be moved from the Chapel of Italy and presented as an 'Omaggio' (tribute) to St. John's Museum.

Malta had already been through a difficult period when, after its restoration in Rome, The '*Beheading of St. John*' had been temporarily moved to the National Museum. Now once again, a religious painting was being moved from a church to a museum. Few seemed to mind but some did complain for a number of reasons.

The '*St. Jerome*' was placed in a small room at the end of a long corridor, which was quite often left unattended. To make matters worse, the bright light coming in from the balcony opposite was most disturbing and the vertical opening of the doorway hardly did justice to the horizontal format of the picture. A jarring salmon pink curtain that hung behind Caravaggio's study of the saint, and the Prussian blue carpet that led up to this Baroque painting, did not improve matters at all. At one time, the curator had put up a glass screen to protect the painting but had been asked to remove it.

The minutes of a St. John's Committee meeting record my motion to inscribe a plaque stating that the '*St. Jerome*' was on loan from St. John's Co. Cathedral. At a later date, the minutes should also include my offer to provide an iron grille to be placed at the entrance to the room that the painting was in. My first motion was acted upon but not the second. It was not that I ever suspected that the painting would be stolen but I was worried that it was not properly supervised and that it might be vandalized - until that terrible evening on the 29th of December in 1984 when Dominic came to the Priory to tell me that the painting had been stolen!

There was little one could do at the time.

Saturday, 29th

I got Dominic to get into his little red car and drove at once to the Police Depot. Once there, we reported the theft and insisted that the airport and harbour be properly supervised to ensure that the painting would not leave the Island. We then drove to the Minister's house, but he was not in so we waited outside in the bitter cold till about midnight. As soon as the Minister arrived we gave him a full account of what had happened.

The Minister has promised to phone me at noon tomorrow. (He did not.)

Sunday, 30th

Sunday!

Dominic and I go to St John's Museum – re Caravaggio. The Archbishop came to the Museum. He wanted to see where the painting had been hanging at the time of the theft. A Monsignor butts in saying, "…These things did not happen when I was in charge!" I shut him up.

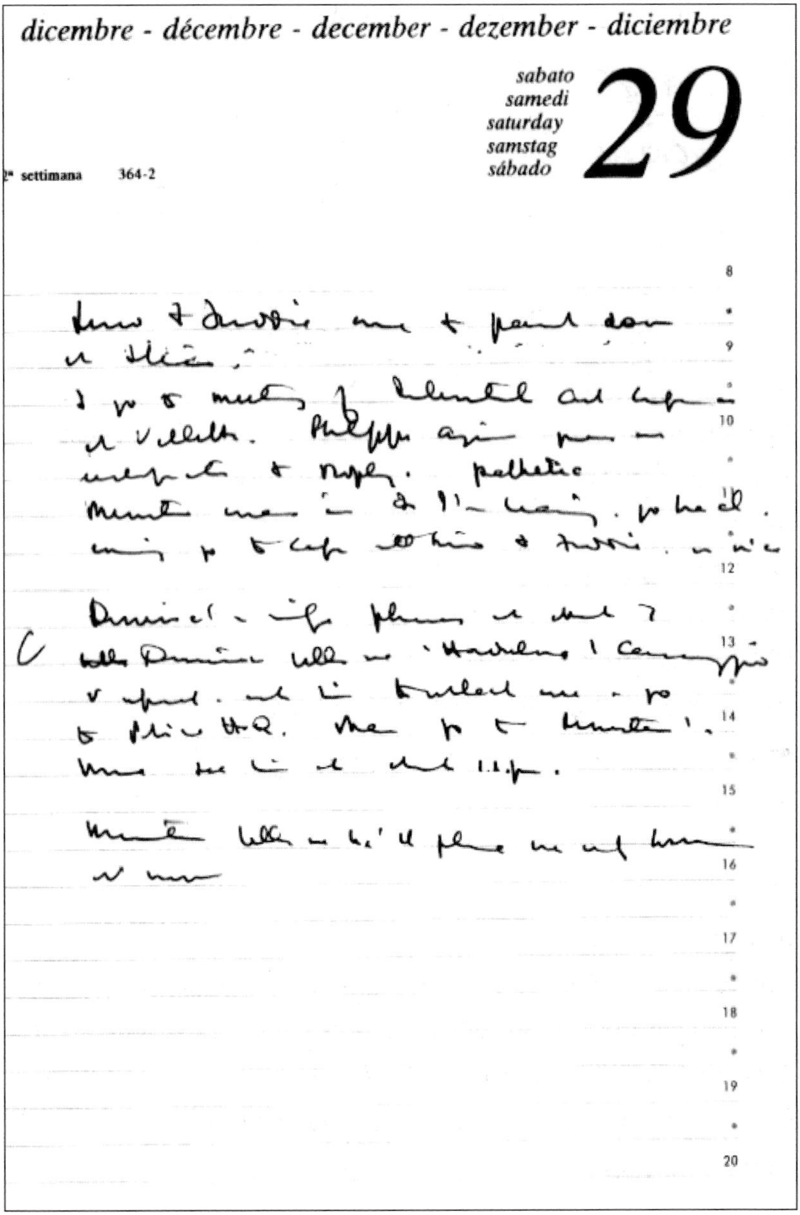
dicembre - décembre - december - dezember - diciembre

sabato
samedi
saturday
samstag
sábado

29

2ª settimana 364-2

8 9 10 11 12 13 14 15 16 17 18 19 20

Monday, 31ˢᵗ

Went to Police Headquarters again this evening. Gave further details.... Took a member of the CID along with us to a friend who worked in the printing trade. We wanted to see whether the placard, 'WORK IN PROGRESS' used in the theft would give us any clues.

We discovered that such notices are quite easily available on the market.

And so 1984 has come to an end. The 'St. Jerome' has disappeared and there seems to be little hope that we will ever see it again.

The first Biennale of Sacred Art - Artists at the Archbishop's Palace

Chapter 3

MINISTERS & MONSIGNORI

Tuesday, 1st

Heavy rains!

Thursday, 3rd

Times of Malta requests information on 'St. Jerome' theft.

Sunday, 6th

Stormy weather!

Tuesday, 8th

Since the real culprit responsible for the theft of the painting cannot be found, it seems one has to be fabricated. There is a search for the proverbial scapegoat. Today at the first St John's Committee meeting held since the theft, I expected that security

The frame of the painting of St. Jerome by Caravaggio, on the floor as it was left by thieves on Saturday afternoon.

Police intensify search for stolen Caravaggio

By a Staff Reporter

An additional motive for Saturday's theft of the priceless Caravaggio painting of St. Jerome was that the artist's works were very much in favour at present with art lovers, an art expert said yesterday.

Artists and their works go through periods when they are ignored, and through others when they are very much in demand. Michelangelo Merisi da Caravaggio (1573-1610) and his

EXCHANGE OF GREETINGS

The President Miss Agatha Barbara will be at the Palace in Valetta today between 12.05 and 1 p.m. to exchange greetings with members of the public who might wish to call on her.

The Prime Minister's visitors' book will be at the Auberge de Castile in Valetta and a copy at the office of the Gozo Secretariat in Victoria, today between 9 a.m. and noon.

The Archbishop will receive members of the public to exchange New Year greetings at the Archbishop's Palace in Valetta between 11.30 a.m. and 12.30 p.m.

Nationalist Party leader Dr. Eddie Fenech Adami will also exchange New Year greetings with members of the public. He will be at the Party's headquarters in

works were at present passing through a very popular phase with lovers of painting, the expert said.

For instance, he pointed out, they were holding in Syracuse, an exhibition of works by Caravaggio which could be found in Sicily, to mark the discovery of one of his paintings, showing St. Lucia, which had been stolen some time ago.

The Caravaggio painting showing St. Jerome naked to the waist sitting on a couch and writing, was stolen from a room at the Museum of St. John's Co-Cathedral in Valetta in a daring robbery soon after the museum opened to the public on Saturday afternoon.

The canvas was neatly cut from the frame which was discovered by the Museum authorities on the floor of the room where the painting was on display.

Police investigators led by CID Superintendent C. Bonello and Inspector J. Psaila, are looking into the possibility that the stolen painting is destined to be taken abroad. In fact the Malta Police have requested the help of the international police organization Interpol, sources close to the Police said yesterday.

The sources added that the Police have carried out various searches locally in effort to trace the painting.

The Times - Tuesday, January 1, 1985

"ST. JEROME" TAKEN ABROAD

POLICE INTENSIFYING SEARCH

Police are no nearer to tracing the stolen Caravaggio painting "St Jerome" than they were a week ago. Sources close to the Police who are intensifying their investigations of the theft, which took place a week ago today, told "The Democrat" that although many leads and theories have been investigated, the police have always run into a "cul-de-sac".

The same sources however told The Democrat that it now appears that the painting has already found its way out of Malta.

It has almost been ascertained that the daring theft took place between 3.20 p.m. and 3.35 p.m. last Saturday. And this would have given ample time for the thieves to catch the Alitalia flight AZ 491 to Rome, which left Malta at 4.30 p.m.

Earlier this week, the Maltese authorities asked Interpol to help in tracing the painting, while Police in Malta are known to have interrogated and arrested some people in connection with the theft. Among those interviewed by Police are some foreigners including two Italians.

Our art correspondent adds:

"St Jerome" (picture) was painted by the world-famous Michelangelo Merisi (1573-1610) while in Malta in 1608. In that year he also painted "Mary Magdalene" which has also been lost.

"St Jerome" is an oils on canvas painting measuring 117 x 157 cm and was restorated in Rome in 1955. The saint is depicted naked to the waist, sitting on a draped couch at a table writing in a book and with his left hand grasping an ink-pot. A skull and a candle-stick are on the table.

Caravaggio also painted a portrait of Alof de Wignacourt which is now at the Louvre in Paris.

"St Jerome" was moved to the Co-Cathedral Museum in Valletta about 15 years ago and was one of the exhibits at the 13th Council of Europe Art Exhibition held in Malta in 1970.

Caravaggio led a notably quarrelsome and disorderly life and in 1606 was exiled from Rome. Grand-Master Wignacourt enticed Caravaggio to Malta where he was commissioned to do a number of paintings, including the three mentioned above as well as "The Sleeping Cupid" now at the Pitti Museum in Florence and perhaps his masterpiece, "The Beheading of St John the Baptist" which can be seen at the Oratory of St John's co-Cathedral.

In July 1608 Caravaggio was admitted as a member of the Order of St John as a Knight of Grace, but he was later imprisoned at fort St Angelo. He escaped in October of that year and returned to Italy. Expelled from the Order in December 1608, he died two years later.

It is relevant to point out that Caravaggio also painted "The Last Supper". This painting was also stolen from Italy some ten years ago.

Many believe that in recent years a new interest in Caravaggio has arisen in the art world and this fuels speculations that the theft of "St Jerome" may be a commissioned work of some foreign art collector.

(see also editorial)

"St Jerome": a great loss to the Maltese nation

The Democrat - Saturday, January 5, 1985

would have been the main item on the agenda. Instead, the Chairman referred to the theft and hinted that if an enquiry were to be held, he would say that orders had been given and these had been disobeyed! Members of the committee sensed the drift and one of them proposed a vote of confidence in the Curator. I seconded this motion immediately. Fingers of blame were still being pointed - so I just stormed out of the meeting. The New Year seems to bring no new hopes.

---

l-orizzont – It-Tlieta, 8 ta' Jannar, 1985

CIAO CARAVAGGIO!

• **LIL** dawk il-barranin li jridu jakkwistaw xi biċċa xogħol tal-arti imprez-zabbli b'xejn, nistiednuhom jiġu Malta. Ma għandhomx minn x'hiex jibżgħu. Jistgħu jidħlu fil-mużewijiet tagħna x'ħin iridu u l-anqas għandhom għalfejn joqogħdu jippjanaw jekk iridu jwettqu xi serqa. Kull ma għandhom bżonn huwa daqsxejn ta' xafra biex jaqtgħu it-tila minn mal-gwarniċ jew inkella daqsxejn ta' djamant biex iqasqsu l-ħġieġ. Għal bqija ma għandhomx għal-fejn iħabblu moħħhom għall-għassa għax meta jkun hemm din żgur li qatt ma tkun stretta.

Thursday, 10th

I have to submit a report to the government on the theft of the painting to the Ministry.

A scapegoat is still being sought. A former Minister had once promised to provide an extra watchman. This never materialized, now they are putting the blame on her.

Saturday, 12th

Police call me to identify some other stolen paintings that have been recovered.

Thursday, 31st

Suddenly everyone seems aware of the prevailing lack of security.

At a St. John's Committee meeting held today at Chairman's residence. Chairman wants all silver in St. John's Co Cathedral to be moved to the sacristy. Members of the committee do not agree.

The silver was moved just the same. As usual, it was a case of 'Chairman vincit, Chairman imperat'.

Monday, 18th

Rumours about various thefts and such happenings are rife. A report from Police Headquarters that the Cathedral Museum has been left open all night.

(In fact it was The Natural History Museum – also in Mdina)

Tuesday, 19th

Police Superintendent Tommasi comes to Fine Arts Museum. He accompanies me to check on gold and silver coin collection - all seems OK.

Wednesday, 20th

Went to Mdina with Supt. to check on Vilhena Palace.

Whilst in the area, thought we had better see that all is well at Norman House. Glad to see that the silver we had moved from the bank to the strong room, there is also safe.

Tuesday, 9th

Meeting at St. John's – annoyed with Mgr. Coleiro for removing silver to sacristy without approval of committee.

ART LOVERS ASSESS CARAVAGGIO THEFT

By a Staff Reporter

Art lovers familiar with the layout of the Cathedral Museum in Valetta are convinced that last Saturday's theft of the Caravaggio painting of St. Jerome was the work of a group of about five persons. They believe they were professional burglars.

While one of the thieves calmly averted the theft from being foiled by telling a German tourist that she could not see the painting as they were working on it, in another section of the corridor the thieves set up a chain with a sign in the middle saying "No entry" in English and Maltese.

ATTENDANT ON LEAVE

The thieves had taken a risk in doing this because a suspicious museum official had every authority to walk past a no-entry sign if he so wished, the sources said. The thieves had however picked a day when one of the attendants was on leave.

One, or more from the group, must have stood guard, while at least two others lowered the painting with its heavy frame.

from the wall.

The painting was neatly cut from the frame. It was then lowered or thrown out, onto St. John's Square from a window behind one of the tapestries adorning the walls.

The painting is likely to have been rolled before being taken out, and tiny shreads of canvas were found near the window, the sources said.

The thieves got away with possibly the biggest and most important theft in Maltese history. The Police are actively investigating the case, the sources said.

'FOREIGN INSTIGATION'

"It was a professional job, obviously made at foreign instigation", an art expert said.

He shared the hope of other art lovers that one day the painting would be found and put back in its place.

"Caravaggio paintings stolen in Sicily have been recovered", he said to add weight to his hopes.

"The thieves may have a problem of getting rid of their haul", an art expert said, pointing out that the painting was "very, very important and therefore well known in museums worldwide".

The thieves will have a difficult job selling it "unless it is for someone who wants to hide it away *for his eyes only*", the art expert said, quoting the title of a James Bond film.

Lira breaks new ground against Sterling

The exchange rate of the Maltese Lira for Sterling yester-

Tuesday, 23rd

Hunt for a scapegoat still on. A Board of inquiry has been set up. They are trusted acquaintances – an Ex-judge and a lawyer - so I have offered to appear before them. At the inquiry this morning I explained that I had never approved of the move of the 'St. Jerome' to the St. John's Museum, but the Chairman had blind trust in the foreign expert who had suggested the move and my words had fallen on deaf ears.

I mentioned the iron grille, which I had offered to provide and also the plaque stating that the 'St. Jerome' was on loan. Also reminded them about the promised custodian.

Got rather worried when the Board asked me the loaded question - "What would you have done - stayed in your office or guarded the paintings?" I explained that the curator in a Museum is not there to act as watchman. I think they understood.

As far as I know the findings of this Board were never made public.

Friday, 13th

Met Renzo Piano at Luqa Airport, took him to the Hypogeum and Tarxien Temples. Then we went to see the Prime Minister. Originally Piano had come to Malta to work on Children's Museum. Prime Minister wants him to work on more serious projects.

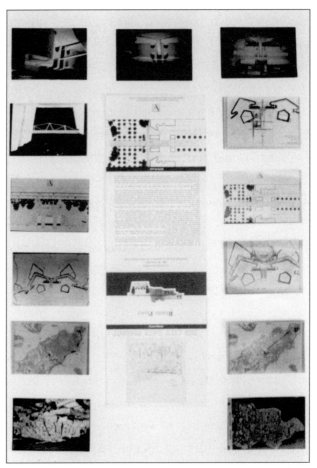

Exhibition of Renzo Piano's Projects held in Quebec City

Tuesday, 22nd

People are taking advantage of the current security scare. Received an odd phone call - a small oil painting attributed to Solimena has gone missing from Fine Arts Museum. Suggest they should search the immediate area thoroughly including behind curtains – some idiot had hidden it behind a curtain, thinking that this would earn him a place in history!

A few weeks later I was told that a person had tried to throw something at the 'Beheading of St. John' in the Oratory and had actually managed to get away.

Other treasures in St. John's Co Cathedral desperately needed protection. At the next St. John's Committee meeting, I insisted that we put up a rope to avoid having visitors walk all over the marble tombstones. Unfortunately, at the time more interest was being shown in a cheap portable altar that had just been put up. One Monsignor was all for it – another promised me anything if I could see to its removal. Later on there was some talk of moving the main altar of St. John (presumably in the name of the liturgical revival). I protested to the Minister and he promised me that this move will be resisted with all the means at our disposal.

The Prime Minister assures me that he is most willing to help with the maintenance and restoration of St. John's Co Cathedral. He is also in agreement that the local association of the Knights of Malta make use of the Church of Our Lady of Victories. He has asked me to draw up points for an agreement regarding this matter.

I informed the Archbishop about all of this, when he came to give the Sacrament of Confirmation at our Church in Sliema.

Tuesday, 31ˢᵗ

"...Ring out the old. Ring in the new...The year is dying...Let it die..."

Another year over. No Caravaggio – Nec spes, nec metus (No hope, yet no fear.)

Chapter 4

MERISI

Friday, 3rd

One of my restorers came to my office to complain that a gecko had crawled out of a crack in the wall while he was restoring a fresco in the Palace. Asked him to put the complaint in writing!

A few days later the same restorer reappeared with his union to back him — this seemed an unfair advantage over the gecko that had no union representative.

Saturday – 5th

Opening of Spinola Palace as a Museum of Contemporary Art.

Band, orchestra, ballet, folk groups. Felt very hot and bothered. Am annoyed with Minister. He thanks his private secretary in public, but forgets to mention the Architect and others responsible for all the work.

Spinola Palace

Friday, 15th

Minister opens the War Room Complex at Lower Lascaris. H.M.S. Brazen in port. Minister dons sailor's cap! Brazen indeed!

Sunday, 17th

Reception on board H.M.S.Brazen.

Saturday, 25th

Came out of my short spell in hospital. Rather fed up of going in and out of hospital and taking all this medication.

> *'Throw physics to the dogs... I'll none of it...'*

The oesteomylitis in my leg has been a nuisance most of the year. Many faithful friends have stood by me and helped me to make it through these dark days.

Little did I realize that it was not only my family and friends who had been eagerly waiting for me to come out of hospital – or for my return to work!

Wednesday, 12th

Back at the Museum after sick leave.

Find total confusion – workers painting walls wrong colour – chocolate brown.

Saturday, 22nd

Feel tired – Visited my good friend and physician Dr. Captur – says I am ok.

Monday, 24th

First full day at work – feeling much better now.

It happened this evening - at 10 to 6 exactly. I had just come back to the priory from work. A young man, with black curly hair and wearing a light blue denim jacket, knocked at my door at the priory and asked to see me. He had an envelope that he wanted to deliver. He said it was from a Mr. Joe Borg. I asked him which Joe Borg was he referring to.

He replied, "He lives next door to me". As I could see that the envelope had 'CONFIDENTIAL' written on it in block letters, I did not push him. I thanked him and he left.

The main reason that I did not persist with the questioning was because there actually was a Joe Borg that I knew very well. This particular Joe Borg was a cousin of mine - his son Mario, of whom I was very fond, had just died. He was an innocent victim of infected blood given him in hospital. As it was obvious that the envelope contained some sort of object, I presumed that his father had sent me a small keepsake of his son. I therefore asked no further questions and my visitor disappeared as quickly as he had come.

I opened the envelope. Inside was a smaller envelope – and there was also a tape cassette. On the smaller envelope were written the words, 'Fader (sic) Do not open this envelope until you have listened to the tape. And when you do listen to the tape, see that you are alone'.

Envelope and tape received by Fr. Zerafa

Of course, the first thing I did was to open the envelope. Inside was a Polaroid photo of the stolen Caravaggio – cut out of its stretcher and lying on the floor with a coffee pot placed on top of it! It all came to me in a flash!

Polaroid photo of the stolen painting

I rushed out of my room and ran downstairs but the young man had disappeared into the crowd outside.

When I came back to my room, I made a rough sketch in pencil just to remind me of what the young man looked like. I then played the tape.

It was serious staff. Someone seemed to be reading a prepared text - I could hear him turning over the pages. The voice told me that 'he' or rather 'they' had the Caravaggio. They had tried to sell the painting in Europe but had not succeeded. They were now about to take it to America - was I interested? They wanted half a million Maltese Liri for it, but there were conditions and he spelt them out one by one. I was <u>not</u> to contact the police. If I did *they would know. Somehow, I felt sure he meant it. I was <u>not</u> to speak to the Press. There was a pause; suddenly the voice turned more solemn. "This is not a joke!" he said, "Jekk tipprova tilghabna jiddispjacik* (If you try to cheat us you will regret it). *...You had better tell us straight away whether you are interested or not..."* [Of course I was interested!] *To drive the point home, the voice proceeded to list a string of very unpleasant things that would befall us should I not comply with their demands. The threats included setting fire to the Tapestries, damaging the works by Mattia Preti, vandalising St. John's and so on and so forth.*

One thing I found, and still find, rather intriguing was that he repeated the phrase "I draw your attention" (to this or to that...) <u>three</u> times. Somehow it sounded like legal jargon – the sort of thing one would expect from a lawyer or a policeman or someone who had connections with the law.

I was terribly excited but also very, very happy - a great painting that had been lost had somehow been found ...

Well, almost found.... Eight long months of worry, disappointment, frustration and disgust were to pass before the agony could turn to ecstasy.

At least the two-year silence has been broken. This tape turning up is the first glimmer of hope that might lead to the recovery of the painting. It is also the challenge of a lifetime. If I fail, I feel it will be the end of me.

But this was only the beginning.

The voice on the tape said that I would be contacted.

He seemed to be trying to impress me - he gave me a password: 'Merisi'. Perhaps 'Merisi' is trying to tell me that he is quite at home with the artist Caravaggio and that he has done his homework well. He said he would contact me in a week's time.

In fact he phoned the very next day, just before noon.

Tuesday - 25ᵗʰ

Spoke to sacristan about yesterday evening. He tells me that there were two men. The man who had been up to my room and another man - a 'well dressed' man - waiting for him.

Just before noon - receive phone call at Museum, "Jien Signor Merisi – ircevejtu l-pakkett?" (I am Signor Merisi, have you received the package?) *I said I had received it.... And yes, I was*

The canvas showing damage and missing bits

interested and that I had been thinking about it ever since and had already made discreet enquiries. Then, in order not to appear too interested, I pointed out that from the photo that they had sent me, the painting seemed to be practically ruined. 'M' hung up.

As soon as my telephone call with Merisi ended I contacted the Ministry of Culture.

At the time it was not easy to get through to my Minister and one had to first get past an all-powerful secretary.

I phoned the Ministry and asked to speak to my Minister. It must have sounded quite urgent – the secretary spoke to me immediately. I asked for the earliest possible appointment with Minister. Secretary asked no further questions.

Am to meet Minister tomorrow early a.m.

Wednesday, 26th

Early this morning Minister and I had a lengthy conversation. I gave him a full account of what has happened so far. I tell him that he is one of the few to know all this and it is absolutely essential to keep things secret. Probably to test me, he asks me for my thoughts on the matter. Tried to impress upon him that this was something of great importance; I say that I believe that they really do have the painting and that it is likely that there is more than one person involved in the plot. The Minister decides the best way forward is to play for time until we can formulate a proper plan of action.

Minister says what a 'scoop' it would be if we found the painting! Hated that word, but then it was the politician talking!

The Minister is to inaugurate an art exhibition later this evening. Tells me that he is considering making an appeal during his opening speech to have the painting returned. Do not know whether he is being serious. Naturally, I advise very strongly against it.

The rest was... silence.

Later on I was to hear that someone had approached Sotheby's branch office in Florence, with a Caravaggio painting for sale but they had not taken the call seriously.

Monday, 1st

I was called to the Minister's office at 3pm. He has certainly not been idle. The Minister introduced me to two Italian officials who have been brought over from Italy for their expertise. I gave them a brief account of all that I knew. Also showed them the Polaroid photo, the envelopes and the tape.

Their first suggestion is that my telephone at the Museum of Archaeology be placed sotto controllo. Should Signor Merisi call again I am to ask for more photos - which should include a newspaper in order to give an indication of a location with an approximate time frame.

I also have to discuss the place of exchange once the money is available. Above all, I am to play for time.

I asked Dominic to come to the Priory where we played the tape over and over. I am still intrigued by certain expressions used and so is Dominic.

Tuesday, 2nd

The two 'experts' that I had met in the Minister's office call at the Museum. They wanted to see where the 'St. Jerome' painting had been hanging before it was stolen. I did not accompany them. I sent them to St. John's Co Cathedral to meet Dominic. I was worried that anyone who might have been following me (and I did get the feeling that I was being watched), would see me with these two Italian police officers. That would have given the game away - straight away! They were both wearing similar raincoats - the kind of raincoats that police detectives wear in films – they could be spotted miles away. That would have been the end of everything! The Italians certainly looked the part but I must admit it made my heart bleed to see the way they were handling the Polaroid and the tape - particularly after I had been so careful not to disturb any fingerprints.

Wednesday, 3rd

Another Merisi phone call. I said it was too soon to tell them anything. Signor Merisi insists on a definite reply – they've had other offers. As advised by the Italian experts, I asked for more photos, which were to include a newspaper displaying the current date. I insist that I be told where the exchange would eventually take place. Emphasised a few times that they must take care of the painting - it was already damaged and the canvas still un-stretched – it had to be treated with the utmost care. I tried to play down its value, saying that it was now worth only half of its original price since it was damaged. And after all it was stolen property! I think this got to them – they promised to send me the photos as asked.

I went back to the Ministry this afternoon. Another meeting with the Italian experts. This time, the Minister for Arts had with him the Minister for Communications as well as a technician. I was asked if I objected to having my phone 'placed under surveillance'. I was assured that this was perfectly legal and that it had been done in the past, 'in the recent past' in fact. Naturally, I had no objection at all.

V. Apap, The Prophet Abdias, Jesus of Nazareth Church, Sliema

Friday, 5ᵗʰ

The Italian experts phoned from Rome this morning to ask me, "Tutto calmo?" I assure them that things are 'too calm'.

Do not really feel myself. Try to look unruffled. When anyone at the Priory notices anything unusual, I just say that I am worried about the Manoel Island Project that I am involved in at the moment.

Saturday, 6ᵗʰ

Appointment with V. Apap.

Had to attempt to look perfectly serene this morning as I posed for the sculptor Vincent Apap. Modelled for a statue of the prophet Abdias for our Dominican Church in Sliema.

No one who sees the statue now, with that angelic smile on its face, can imagine the hell I was going through at the time.

As far as I was concerned, things were 'tutto calmo'. But 'Tutto calmo' did not mean 'tutto fermo'. Things were not at a standstill.

Father Provincial is on his official visitation to our Priory. A very serious occasion - can be quite unpleasant. Obviously cannot tell Father Provincial much about the 'Caravaggio affair' although he is a good father and friend. He is very appreciative of my work and I actually feel rather encouraged after his visit.

(I do sometimes wonder why my senior Superiors have always been so good to me while the minor ones can be so annoying?!) But... I digress.

Apart from my dealings with Merisi et al, I was involved in the Manoel Island project and holding regular meetings with the Prime Minister. This was very time consuming, but working closely with the Prime Minister was an experience as well as a pleasure.

Tuesday, 9th

Meet Italian Prince Emanuele di Savoia and the experts involved in the Manoel Island project.

Project OK. To preserve Fort and Lazaretto. Chapel to be restored and used as Inter-Denominational Centre. Conservation of the stone could be carried out by our restoration students.

Wednesday, 10th

The Prince comes to the museum. Had lunch with him at the Hilton Hotel followed by a meeting at Malta Development Corporation re M.I. project.

Thursday, 11th

The telephone expert comes to 'fix' phone in my office. A brave attempt to trace the phone calls! I know nothing about telephones. Get the impression that few people do. I never know what is really happening or whether all the contraptions that are fitted from time to time, are in fact, producing any results.

Friday, 12th

Come home from work to find an envelope with the Polaroid photos

I had requested from Sig. M. There is also the promised piece of canvas.

Monday, 15th

I showed this first piece of tangible evidence to the Minister. The canvas had a special kind of lining that had been used when the painting was first restored in Rome. Told the Minister I had no doubt at all that this was 'our' Caravaggio.

This afternoon another phone gadget installed in my room at the Priory.

Pieces of canvas cut from the painting - mafia style

Tuesday, 16th

M. calls. He gives me two weeks to make a decision. I tell him that their asking price is too high. They want to know how much we are prepared to pay. Begin to feel that we are getting somewhere. Insist on knowing place of exchange. They say they won't tell me now but will send me a tape with instructions when we have the money and they bring the painting back from Italy!

Seems the painting is not in Malta and will not be brought back until we really talk money.

Tarxien Room at the Museum of Archaeology coming along nicely. Consider this an important room in the Museum and we must make a success of it. Told by Ministry that we cannot afford 8 spotlights at one go – we must order 4 this year and 4 the next. (!)

Wednesday, 17th

Speech following budget day.

I was present in Parliament. No opposition Members attended. My Minister - for Foreign Affairs and Culture - spoke mainly about foreign contacts and made a passing reference to vandalism.

Phone out of order.

Many Maltese will remember how primitive our telephone system was at this time. Telephones were often out of order. In a way this gave me some respite from the daily phone calls from Signor Merisi.

No sooner was my phone repaired than Signor Merisi was calling again. Quite often I had nothing to say, so I would tell him that

I had people in my office and would he please phone some other time. My secretary became quite good at keeping him at bay. Merisi's main interest was in obtaining a 'cifra' (an amount) from me. He maintained this insistence.

As a rather mixed blessing, at around this time, I had to be admitted to St. Luke's Hospital for medical treatment and this also saved me from having to reply straight away to M's demands.

Thursday, 18th

The phones at the Priory and in my office at the Museum are constantly being 'seen to'. Another earphone and some sort of switch is the latest intervention in a series of installations. Every

Fr. Zerafa's office at the Museum

previous contraption seems not to have worked though the technician does his best. I've never had much knowledge of, or faith in, these mechanical toys. Must confess - feel they are a waste of time.

Friday, 19th

Meeting of Antiquities. Committee threatens to resign as they feel that a mockery is being made of what the Committee stands for.

Wednesday, 24th

Very heavy rains. Went to museum. Lots of people arrive with Christmas presents. Rainwater leaked through library roof.

Come home to Priory at 3 pm. Confessions, Christmas Carols and Midnight Mass.

Friday, 26th

Phone repaired after three days. More people with more presents. Merisi phones. Tell him to phone later - lots of people in my office. M mentions 'cifra' again.

In a way this was ridiculous. Imagine me, a Dominican Friar with a vow of poverty and absolutely no sense of the value of money, dealing in thousands of Liri, as though I were Henry Ford himself! And all along, of course, I knew that the Government never had the slightest intention of forking out a single cent!

Saturday, 27th

Last injection. Can stop taking the antibiotics. Thank God.

Monday, 29th

Technician comes to check phone. Again gadget does not work. Fixes switch and earphone.

Afternoon party for kids at De Porres Hall. Minister is present at party. He wants 200 statuettes of the famous Sleeping Lady ... and a report on Caravaggio.

Show him portrait that I had painted of Fr.Born (founder of the De Porres Hall).

We moved the original statuette of the Tarxien Sleeping Lady to a more prominent and secure place. Now visitors to the Museum of Archaeology can see it 'in the round' as they go into the Temple Room, or go downstairs to the proposed New Exhibition Hall.

Tuesday, 30th

At 11 am I received another M. phone call. We talk money and I again say that his price is ridiculous. Some heated haggling. He finally accepts offer of Lm35,000. I ask about place of exchange. M. still insists on exchange taking place in Malta. Tells me he will send tape. Wonder what they have in mind?

Have been trying to prolong conversations on the phone with M. as much as possible. The idea is to give the technician time to trace the call.

Later on, I would come to know that this involved a risk to my life, but at the time I was blissfully unaware of it. I insisted on having the exchange take place in Florence for various reasons. I had spent the happiest time of my life there and I knew the main and back streets of Florence better than I knew those of Sliema. Besides, in Florence we would have the help of the Italian police, whereas in Malta the Prime Minister is adamant that the Maltese police are to be kept out altogether!

Wednesday, 31st

Today we had our first breakthrough! The call has been traced to the Zejtun area! I was overjoyed until I was told that the area could also include the entire Cottonera district - which means it could be practically anywhere. This seems to be as far as we can get. High Tech indeed! My Minister wants a full report on this.

As one can see, I had little help. Later on I would hear someone on TV saying how he had directed me and told me to inform the thieves that he was getting the money through a vote in Parliament. This was more than news to me! It would have been an interesting contribution at the time except that like so many other claims, it was just not true. By the time I actually met this person, I had been dealing with the thieves for eight months and had been telling them a very different story as to how we were hoping to get the money for the painting.

Chapter 5

PROJECTS & PLANS

The New Year started with the return of an old problem. Surgery on my knee, undergone in London some years back, had seemed successful thanks to the fine doctors and nurses and the loving care of my brother. Now the 'old knee' was playing up again - I had to be admitted to St. Luke's Hospital in Malta for treatment.

Friday, 2nd

A Minister phones re restoration of Santo Spirito Hospital in Mdina. Tell him that I'm very interested.

Lost interest when I heard that he had insisted on having Carrara Marble in the Old Chapel instead of the hardstone that the committee had agreed on.

Wednesday, 7th

Back at work.

Friday, 9th

This morning I heard from Signor Merisi for the first time this year. I had absolutely nothing to report so I said that I had visitors, and asked him to phone back some other time. This situation is becoming impossible. If the Government does not take a decision soon, Merisi is bound to get suspicious. I can't hold him off much longer. We need a proper plan as well as the help of the local police force if the exchange is going to take place in Malta.

Monday, 12th

Another M. phone call at noon. Asks for assurance that we mean business. He makes it clear that he wants the exchange to take place in Malta.

Telephone technician informs me that buzzer for phone has not worked.

Went to the Ministry. Seems German Embassy is interested in the Auberge de Baviere.

Friday, 16th

Meeting at Curia re Hal-Millieri frescos. Speak to Archbishop about Caravaggio. Archbishop still worried that history will repeat itself. I assure him that there is no talk of that. The 'St. Jerome' will return to St. John's Co Cathedral. He assures me that he has full confidence in me and in what I am doing. He just wanted to make sure that the painting will not go astray – whenever it is actually found!

Monday, 19th

Staff situation at Museum is odd. What we ask for we don't get -

but we do get what we don't want.

Tuesday, 20th

Meeting at Mnajdra Temples with Curator of Archaeology and Museum Architect. Discuss protection around Mnajdra. Suggest an iron fence following the lay of the land. The Curator and I prepare drawings.

Merisi phoned again but my secretary told him I was in a meeting. This time it was true. I was with Prince Vittorio Emanuele and his experts working on the Manoel Island project.

This was one of two main projects going on at the time; the other project being the reconstruction of Valletta's 'City Gate'.

Renzo Piano, one of the greatest living architects, was working

Photomontage of Manoel Island project autographed by Prince and Prime Minister

on his comprehensive plan for Valletta and some of the meetings were held in my office at the Auberge de Provence in Republic Street.

Piano was a most creative and innovative architect. Somebody actually compared his visit to Caravaggio's stay in Malta! The fact that he was here, as well as working on the plan for our capital city, should have been a great honour for Malta. We had numerous meetings with the Prime Minister and with the Chamber of Architects. The plan was strenuously opposed. As usual the problem was not so much with the project as with the personalities involved - with the singers, not with the song.

Wednesday, 21st

Meeting at Prime Minister's office. Discussed Valletta project, Baviere and Manoel Island.

Thursday, 22nd

Morning meeting at MDC (Malta Development Corporation) re Fort Chambray... Evening meeting - 9pm with Chamber of Architects.

Monday, 26th

Minister's secretary phones to say 'Children's Museum' has got to be ready by Election Day. He's playing God again! I had a lot of respect and affection for my Minister but often had problems with the set up at the Ministry. The Minister was taken up with Foreign Affairs and the Museums were left to the mercy of political animals. They thought they were helping the Minister – they certainly did not help the Museums. My staff would be taken to carry out work unconnected with the Museums. A political exhibition that I had objected to was put up while I was away.

Tuesday, 27th

Merisi phones me at the Priory. Tell him everyone is thinking of elections. He will have to wait till it is all over.

Thursday, 5th

I received an envelope with another cassette tape at the Priory. A rather ominous message. "You have been dragging on for too long. The Italians do not care at all about your elections. It is not true that the value of the painting has decreased because it is damaged. It had been restored in the past and can be restored again!"

I just can't take any more risks. I told the telephone technician that we had to do something – he obliged by installing another gadget.

Merisi phoned again. To play for time, I told him that I was occupied in a committee meeting.

Feeling desperate – no official advice or direction forthcoming, all attempts to trace the calls have so far failed. Yet in my heart of hearts I feel that by holding firm, I can put them on the defensive and perhaps manage to corner them.

Detail of 'St. Jerome' after restoration

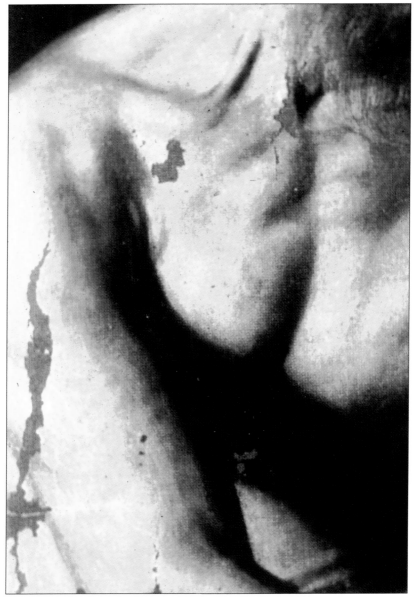

Detail of damaged painting before restoration

Friday, 13th

Receive another tape by mail. A repetition of last week's message.

Wednesday, 18th

Yet another gadget installed at the Priory!

Friday, 20th

At 10.30 a.m. I received a phone call from Signor Merisi - I showed surprise that he could not understand that everyone had election fever. I asked him - was he not living in Malta like the rest of us? This really annoyed him and he said he would give me until the end of March. After that the painting would be taken to America. I shouted back they would not sell it. He insisted that they would not wait any longer. I told him that I would not deal with them under threat.

"As a priest I advise you to go to confession, as a Maltese I would tell you to return it to where it belongs."

I pretended to be really angry with the lot of them and he backed off.

In fact my great fear was that they would take advantage and come to me for confession. That would have made my situation very awkward.

Tuesday, 24th

The only sensible words that I heard at this time came from a lawyer I had known for years. He had come to see me and recommended that I get help from a reputable ex CID officer. It seemed to be a sensible idea. I was on my own – I could not chase the thieves or in any way give the impression that I was following them or trying to trap them. They knew who I was. They were probably following my every move.

I put the idea of the CID Officer to the Minister. He shot it down at once. "Why involve an outsider?" Again he repeated, "Let it be! – the Prime Minister has something in mind."

But this *something* was never revealed to me! Looking back, this outsider's experience would have been very helpful.

I also put forward the suggestion that we seek help from our Italian neighbours. These 'foreign collectors' could put an advert in our local papers, announcing their interest in antique paintings for sale. Signor Merisi, having given up hope of further dealings with us, would try to explore this other possibility - and more than likely take the bait.

This idea suffered the same fate as all suggestions not coming from on high – it was shot down - and I had to struggle on.

Thursday, 26th

We heard from the Italian police experts today. They phoned to inform us of the kind of typewriter that had been used to write the first letter. They also told us that the photo had been taken with a common Polaroid camera ...The official report, however, was yet to come through the Embassy!

Never had so many... waited so long for so little...

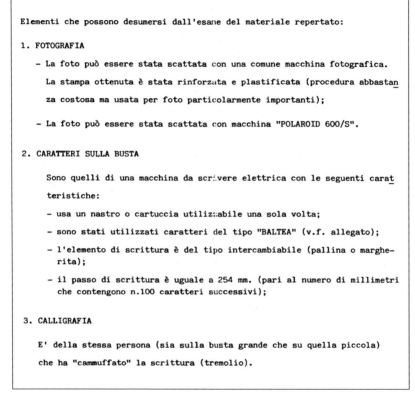

Elementi che possono desumersi dall'esame del materiale repertato:

1. FOTOGRAFIA

   - La foto può essere stata scattata con una comune macchina fotografica.
     La stampa ottenuta è stata rinforzata e plastificata (procedura abbastan
     za costosa ma usata per foto particolarmente importanti);

   - La foto può essere stata scattata con macchina "POLAROID 600/S".

2. CARATTERI SULLA BUSTA

   Sono quelli di una macchina da scrivere elettrica con le seguenti carat
   teristiche:
   - usa un nastro o cartuccia utilizzabile una sola volta;
   - sono stati utilizzati caratteri del tipo "BALTEA" (v.f. allegato);
   - l'elemento di scrittura è del tipo intercambiabile (pallina o marghe-
     rita);
   - il passo di scrittura è uguale a 254 mm. (pari al numero di millimetri
     che contengono n.100 caratteri successivi);

3. CALLIGRAFIA

   E' della stessa persona (sia sulla busta grande che su quella piccola)
   che ha "cammuffato" la scrittura (tremolio).

Official Report sent by Italian Police re typewriter and photo

Signor Merisi, on the other hand, was quite generous with his missives - I had already received a number of envelopes containing tapes.

It was not unknown at the time for letter bombs to be sent to political adversaries and I was half expecting to receive one myself. If the thieves discovered that I had more or less been leading them on, they might try to take their revenge...

Monday, 2nd

I ask a friend, who works at the Post Office, whether any checks for letter bombs are ever carried out. He says that this protection is reserved solely for VIPs. I am obviously expendable so I'll have to think up my own security methods.

Monday, 9th

A Public Works Technical Officer has been sent to the Museum to assist our contractor. I tell him we never did have a contractor. I am told "...give him a chair and he will sit there – orders from on high.".

Saturday, 14th

This morning I received a bulky envelope. Convinced that there was something suspicious inside. Took the envelope on the roof of the Priory, attached strings to the corners and pulled the envelope apart from a distance. Nothing happened! It was just another tape from M and Co. and I've survived to tell the tale.

Friday, 20th

I met the Minister at Joseph Briffa's art exhibition. Spoke about the stolen painting. Told him that something had to be done – and soon! He repeats the usual refrain, "The Prime Minister does not want to involve the Malta Police."

Wednesday, 25th

Another phone call from Merisi. Have nothing to tell the man. Said I was busy and asked him to phone back at 10:00 am tomorrow. Immediately contacted the technician and asked him to be ready to monitor the call at 10 o'clock tomorrow.

Thursday, 26th

Merisi phoned at 10 am as he said he would. The technician was standing by, as agreed, but nothing came of it. How long was I expected to go on baiting Merisi till someone could pinpoint his exact whereabouts?

I am really running out of excuses.

In fact I had already run out of excuses! It is shocking to say this, but a blessing in disguise came with the outbreak of a fire at the Mediterranean Conference Centre in Valletta. A laser beam had apparently been left on which had burnt the stage curtains, and the fire had spread through the whole Conference Centre.

Friday, 27th

Merisi phoned. I played up the damage at the Conference Centre – I said that because of the expense Government had incurred, it would delay matters. It was a very tenuous excuse but I tried to make the most of it – it seemed to work.

Wednesday, 8th

I went with another technician to study the telephone system at the Telephone Exchange at Spencer Hill in Marsa.

It all looked too complicated. If the technician could do nothing, what was I expected to do? Perform a miracle? Who said the age of faith was over?

It was not unusual to be asked to work miracles in Malta. Around this time we had problems with the Triton fountain in Valletta.

The upper basin had been almost totally wrecked when it had been used as a platform for motorcycles during a 'cultural' event!! The fountain with its broken basin presented a pitiful sight. Everyone was complaining.

The resident British artist Victor Pasmore tried to help by writing a letter to the press. This was not appreciated and he was asked to keep out of it.

A visiting card arrived from the Minister with the simple message, 'Mario see that the fountain starts working again!' I was getting quite used to these cryptic messages but this one was quite a masterpiece.

(I still have this card!).

In order to see that something be done about the restoration of the Valletta fountain, I arranged a meeting with the sculptor Censu Apap and the Minister. The Minister insisted that the work be carried out by the state ship repair yard so as to protect local industry. The Malta Dry-docks, however, declined the offer saying that it was impossible to balance the basin on the hands of the tritons in the manner that the artist had originally created it. It was suggested that the sculptor be asked to produce something to support the basin – so he modelled a number of dolphins, which he thought would be in keeping with the idea of tritons. It was a good solution, but then the dolphins were considered unsuitable – a Minister decided that they carried political connotations (they had featured in the national crest used by the previous Government), and so were disqualified. The artist had to come up with another solution – seagulls! At least they soared high above politics.

These interludes I think deserve to be recorded. First of all they show that I was not just a part-time detective trying to outwit Signor Merisi – I was a full time Director of Museums, running a Government department and what was worse, I also had to be at the beck and call of the Minister. '*Ministering to Ministers*' – I called it.

These episodes actually provided me with some light relief - they offered a welcome change from the Caravaggio saga that was killing me with worry and frustration. I would not have survived without the help of God and a strong sense of humour.

Tuesday, 14th

During one of our regular meetings with the Prime Minister about the Manoel Island Project, I managed to get him to one side and brought up the question of the stolen Caravaggio. I got the impression that he was not properly briefed about it - but he was still of the opinion that the Italian police should deal with it as they had more experience. When I asked the PM about the exchange taking place in Malta, he agreed that in that case the Maltese police could be brought in to help. At least he has authorised me to say that the ransom money is available.

Thursday, 16th

I was invited by the Prime Minister to his office at the Auberge de Castille to be present for the signing of the Manoel Island project. Prince Vittorio Emanuele and the Princess were present for the occasion.

We drank champagne and I was given a large photomontage with the whole project signed by the Prime Minister and by the Prince. As I was sitting next to the Prime Minister he showed me a photo showing another part of the project. A modern bridge designed by the Chinese to link both sides of the harbour. He wondered whether the Antiquities Board would accept it. I said it certainly deserved to be studied.

I was very keen on the Manoel Island project - I felt we had done something for Malta. Unfortunately it was not to be.

Wednesday, 22nd

Working on a new project very close to my heart - the construction of an underground gallery at the Archaeological Museum.

Given the limited area at the museum, in order to gain space one had to either go up or dig down. It was not easy to build higher in Valletta so an alternative solution had to be found.

When I had been turning Admiralty House into a Museum of

Fine Arts, way back in 1974, I was lucky enough to have a Minister who trusted me and was genuinely interested in getting things done; She hated red tape as much as I did, she was rough and tough, but she was hard working and honest. I wish I could say the same for some of the people around her.

The ensuing results are still there for all to see. Admiralty House had been used as a residence and office of Commander in Chief Mediterranean for over a hundred years then left abandoned for ten years with a watchman building boats in the courtyard. The fire staircase has been altered to make room for the admiral's orchestra. Rooms were split up, doorways opened, others closed. Each room had a fireplace and a huge military fan. It was good that the architects had been on strike for months. My good friend Dr. Butigieg gave me the men I needed to do the job. An open terrace was turned into a lovely room where we were able to exhibit the Sciortino Bequest for the first time after so many years. Two rooms were built on the roof to house bequests by the artists George Borg and Joseph Briffa. The Monetarium too, was most impressive. The courtyard had been partially built over during the British period to provide bathrooms. I had these additions knocked down. Underneath the courtyard was a huge cistern; the damp rising from the water in it made it impossible to exhibit works of art in the ground floor rooms. I decided to empty the cistern. That solved the problem of the damp but then I had to think of how I would make use of such a magnificent space.

At one time we were holding an exhibition by a Dutch sculptor, a friend of the Minister of Works. At the opening, I appealed for any assistance that could be given to complete the project; the Italian Military Mission responded and showed their willingness to participate in the project. At no cost to the Government, they built a spiral staircase going down to the cistern, had the place paved and provided de-humidifiers. We placed a member of showcases there and displayed a permanent exhibition of gold and silver coins of the Order of St. John.

BROADLANDS,
ROMSEY,
HAMPSHIRE.
SO5 9ZD.

TELEPHONE
ROMSEY (0794) 513333

18 March 1977

Dear Father Zarofa,

Thank you so much for showing me round my old home in South Street. You really have made it into a beautiful museum and I do congratulate you.

I think it very important that there should be an historic link with the previous occupiers of the house, and am so glad you agree.

Yours sincerely,

Mountbatten of Burma

I think it is a pity that this is no longer open to the public.

The careful conversion of Admiralty House into the Museum of Fine Arts in 1974 proved successful. I was pleased to hear that Lord Mountbatten had experienced his satisfaction in a letter to the PM. On a visit to Malta he referred to the Museum with nostalgia as 'his' house. He looked around and said "I don't recognize the place". He later congratulated us in a letter.

As Director of Museums, my office was now at the Auberge de Provence. I now had to deal with another challenge. The courtyard at the Fine Arts had been a fine space for exhibitions but I thought we could have something larger and more accessible at the Archaeology Museum – occupying, as it did, such a central spot in our capital city.

At the time of the Knights, this Auberge had been a self-contained entity. It had dining rooms and sleeping quarters, but also had stables, wine cellars and so on. When the Auberge became the Union Club, the cellars were naturally used as wine cellars and storerooms. After the British left, these cellars were filled with marble slabs, inscriptions and above all material obtained from tombs during archaeological excavations. It was rat infested and the material needed sifting and classifying. I discussed the matter with the Curator of Archaeology and we decided to go ahead. The Minister gave his tacit approval. There were structural problems as there were no proper stairs leading down to the cellars. As with every new project, there was a lot of opposition. New ideas frightened people who felt safe doing nothing.

Monday, 27ᵗʰ

There was a phone call from Merisi today at 12.15. I wanted to make sure that he would keep in contact so I told him that I had good news for him – things were moving. I told him that I was moving too – to a new office.

In fact I was not going anywhere. I was just having a new telephone line and number installed which, we hoped, would make it easier to trace any incoming calls.

A recorded phone message said, *"Fr Zerafa is now in a new office with a new telephone number".*

This was a considerable risk but fortunately Signor Merisi et al seemed to have suspected nothing.

The new 'phone line, as well as the plan, has worked! The call has been traced to a hotel in Marsascala.

Elated …until I am told that the call has come from one of the public phone booths at the hotel. Unless I can get someone to go and watch each of these phone booths, it is going to be useless. Obviously I cannot go myself.

M. phoned again at 12.22. I kept him talking for a while. Then in order to sound optimistic, I said that I was now authorized to tell him that the sum that they had asked for was available. I could tell that this went down well. M. said that they would be bringing the painting back from abroad. Some progress at long last!

Saturday, 2nd

The next few weeks were mad. Election fever had gripped the island and the usual election gimmicks left little time for serious work.

We opened the so-called Children's Museum in of all places, Rudolph Street, Sliema. I introduced the Minister and said that this Museum had been his idea from start to finish.

Monday, 4th

This morning I went with Dominic to the Ministry for Social Services to try to get the personnel information (workbooks) of the staff employed at the Marsascala Hotel.

General elections are only one week away. Perhaps that is why the messenger would not let us see the Minister unless we gave him a good reason why. Perhaps he thought we needed a favour - a job maybe. We waited at the Ministry for two hours, then left.

Just got back to the Priory and the Minister for Social Services has just phoned to ask me what I wanted. Am so annoyed that I have told him to forget it.

Tuesday, 5th

I related what had happened yesterday with the Minister for Social Services to my Minister. He was not pleased that I had sought assistance in another Ministry. He thought that too many people would get to know what was happening.

Saturday, 9th

Election Day. I voted in Valletta even though I had moved to Sliema. So fed up with politics and politicians that I decided to vote for a friend whom, at least, I feel I could trust.

As for the rest – 'a curse on both your houses'.

The election results brought about a change of Government but also the usual demonstrations in Republic Street. I was at the door to see that no harm would come to the Museum of Archaeology. A rough type on a truck shouted insults. He spotted me and shouted that I would never be posing in photographs with the Minister again! I do not know who he was. Unfortunately, I did have to pose with the Minister again!

I was grateful that working on the new exhibition hall at the Museum of Archaeology took up so much of my time and relieved me somewhat from political animals and thieves.

Monday, 11th

The new Government has brought about no extraordinary changes so far - except for an urgent phone call from the Ministry to remove photos of the previous Minister. Members and hangers-on of the party now in power became a nuisance, in place of the others who had been nuisances before them. One particularly unpleasant type at the Museum arrogantly requested to see his file, believing that I had written all sorts of things against him. His ego was obviously deflated when he realized that he had, in fact, been ignored and his record was just a blank. He then insisted on an enquiry "to see why the previous Minister had ordered 200 plaster models of the 'Sleeping Lady'."

This is the stuff that Maltese politics are made of. I am far more interested in retrieving the Caravaggio.

Friday, 15th

A lecture on Caravaggio at the United States Information Service at Floriana attracted huge crowds, but the only thing of interest turned out to be the title.

The new Government was settling in. An architect friend of mine was asked to see to the décor of the Prime Minister's office. I was asked to help. We were given a free hand, and I feel we did a good job. The Prime Minister was duly appreciative

Finished furnishing the Prime Minister's office. Bought an antique ivory crucifix, and hung an old copy of a painting by Guido Reni which I brought from my office. Also provided a fine carpet, a chandelier and lovely plants. Took one of the paintings home to restore myself.

Monday, 18th

Today my new Minister visited the Museum. I told him we had lots of problems at the Museum but the most urgent one was the recovery of the Caravaggio painting, the saga of which has been going on for far too long.

I have known the Minister since we were children; our families have been close friends. He and his brother had come to my ordination reception when I came to Malta for two days, after my ordination in Rome. On my desk at the Priory I still have a mother of pearl crucifix with the Roman Basilicas that he had given me for the occasion. I used to enjoy meeting him and another MP when they visited the Museum of Fine Arts during their free time. They were practically the only MPs that were interested in activities at the museum.

I thought that this Minister's cultural background would stand him in good stead as Minister for Culture and I had all sorts of ideas that I thought he would find exciting and that we could work on together. I enjoyed our conversation and especially our travels together. I always felt he treated me better than I deserved, although some of the things he did, I just could not understand.

Anyway, first and foremost we had to get the painting of the 'St. Jerome' back.

I suggest to my new Minister that we contact the ex CID officer who had been recommended to me. I also repeat my suggestion of placing an advert in the press requesting old paintings, and wait to see whether anything will come of that. I asked him about involving the Italians in this plan. The Minister did not say no – but am not sure that he means 'yes'.

Naturally, I also mentioned our other numerous problems – the various committees having trouble, the situation at the School of Arts and the necessity to organise inventories of works of art when Ministries were being moved.

I suggested that a guide in each of the main museums should

be assigned to look after visiting students. Hundreds of school children visited the Archaeology and Fine Arts Museum with, more often than not, no proper guide. I considered this rather a waste of time and thought that since the same Minister had both the Museums and Education department under his care, it ought to be a fairly straightforward matter to solve - or so I thought.

After this lengthy discussion I was asked to submit a written report! This reminded me of what Karl Marx had said about Blue Books commissioned by the House of Commons.

I was also asked to 'rehabilitate' a party member at the Museum. Later on there would be second thoughts. I would be advised again and again to be on my guard against the "little devil" at my heels.

They say, some are born wise, some achieve wisdom, some have wisdom thrust upon them.

I could appreciate, though, that the Minister did take the Caravaggio issue seriously.

During a reception at the American Embassy, the secretary from the previous Ministry joked about not being able to send more 'rubbish' to the Museum. It had been the policy to load the Museum with unpleasant characters or misfits they did not want. What was worse was that, for years the Museums had been manned by Foreign Office personnel in disgrace, usually political exiles. And they still called it the Ministry for Culture!! So much for culture!

Wednesday, 20th

The phone rang this morning at 9.45 a.m. I noticed that it was not M but a new voice speaking. I assured him that everything was fine but things had been slightly held up because of the recent change of Government...

The Minister sent for me as he wanted a small crucifix to hang up in his office. He told me that he had just been to visit his cousin (the ex Prime Minister), who was in hospital after having suffered a heart attack. They had discussed the stolen Caravaggio and mentioned the possibility of Italian police intervention. I pointed out that an Italian intervention might not work out so well in Malta, and he seemed to agree.

That evening I called a post-election staff meeting. I was very proud of my staff, they were loyal and apart from one negligible exception, I knew that I could rely on them. I reminded them that I had offered to resign when I had had too much interference in the past and I hoped that things would now improve.

Friday, 22nd

Phone call from Signor Merisi at 11.20 a.m. I told him I was in a meeting. He phoned again at 12.20 and at 1.15 p.m. I insisted that this was a new Government administration that was still finding its feet. We had a long argument and he finally promised to wait until the end of the month.

I went to the Ministry to make sure that they were aware of the latest developments in our dealings with Merisi. Post election antics are still evident.

The Curator of Archaeology received an aggressive phone call from my 'little man' at the museum. Now that his party was in power he felt cheeky enough to threaten to smash all the tinted glass that had been recently installed.

Thursday, 28th

We had an exhibition for the first time under the auspices of the new Government. A very good attendance. I felt relieved that political influences did not seem too evident – at least not on the surface.

The new gallery – an exhibition of drawings and models by Renzo Piano

Monday, 1st

This morning at 11.45, Signor Merisi was 'once more unto the breach'. He sounded very determined and said "I'm going to phone on Wednesday for the final transaction. If you don't give me a definite reply I will not phone again." I almost sympathized with him. I said: "It's up to you. I have done my very best and there is little else that I can do."

Wednesday, 3rd

Phone call at 12.43 which I thought was Signor Merisi himself – it was not. I noticed that this was the new voice with a slight stammer. I told him that I was doing my very best. He replied, "I'll give you till next week otherwise I'll do things my own way." I am really worried. How much longer can we delay matters?

Thursday, 4th

Today we held a big exhibition by the famous artist, Maccari, in the Salon of the Museum of Archaeology, followed by dinner at the Casino Maltese. I sat next to the Italian Ambassador so that I would have his full attention and could relate the recent Caravaggio story to him. He was quite appreciative and gave me the names of people at the Italian Embassy whom I could contact for any help I might need.

I spoke to the Minister about the Caravaggio and insisted on doing something about the painting. He told me that he had spoken to the new Minister of Communications. Apparently since there

Maccari Exhibition at the Museum of Archaeology

was now a new *Government*, a brand new technician had to be brought in!

Friday, 5th

At long last I received news that one of the calls has been traced to a shoe factory in Marsa in the south of the Island. This last technician has managed to achieve what we have been attempting for so long. I felt I have to follow it up. I immediately asked my driver to take me to visit a specific area in Marsa. My driver was from Marsa; he knew Marsa well, in fact he knew everybody in Marsa. He knew everything about everybody in Marsa. What he did not know he could always make up. He did know a lot about the people who worked at the shoe factory and what he told me was very useful.

Things are looking up. The voices on the phone begin to assume some shape; they are people I can visualize and size up.

Wednesday, 10th

One of Merisi's men phoned me at 11.05. I told him that everything was going to be alright – I was absolutely sure of that myself - but did not know when, and did not know how, things would fall into place. One more time I suggested to the Minister that we should advertise in the papers for old paintings with the intention of luring Merisi et al into our midst. I thought that this would provide a safe ending with no danger of anyone getting hurt. I also requested to have the workbooks of the employees at the factory in Marsa.

Monday, 15th

New Government Ministers are still settling into their new offices. They continue to call me for advice re interior decoration; infact, to borrow paintings from the Museum.

At 9.50 there was the new man from the Merisi team on the phone. I tried to prolong the conversation. I told him that I had noticed the new voice. Why the change? The new voice answered that they were 'working together'. I pretended that I had my doubts as to whether he really was who he said he was, and asked him about our previous contacts. He answered all my questions accurately. At one point Sig. Merisi himself joined in and said that from now on this second person would be taking over. He seemed quite satisfied with our conversation and told me that the painting would be brought back from Italy within one week.

Tuesday, 23rd

Another call at 11.25 from the new Merisi contact who had 'taken over'.

Finally the workbooks from the shoe factory had arrived. At last! Now I had the details and photos of the people working at the factory - some of whom may have been phoning me almost every day. I looked at the staff details. There were five girls, but the voices had all been male. Out of the four men two had to be chosen. I asked Dominic to come to the Priory and look over this information with me. I noticed that one of the men had 'Returned Migrant' stamped in his work book. The face somehow matched the voice I knew so well. It was just a hunch, meaningless in itself, but it helped to narrow the field of enquiry.

Saturday, 27th

Today for some reason the technician changed the gadget again. This was all beyond me but now I was satisfied that at least we were getting somewhere. At a reception at St. John's Co Cathedral, the Archbishop asked about the stolen Caravaggio. I told him to pray, things were looking up.

I always had a good relationship with him and felt sure that his prayers would certainly carry more weight than mine.

Tuesday, 30th

M. calls at 8.45. Told him I was busy.

M. calls again at 11.00 and at 1.00 p.m. He tells me he's definitely bringing painting from abroad.

14th century cloister at S. Marco in Florence restored and used for contemporary exhibitions

Wednesday, 1st

At 9.20 the 'second voice' called. He described his part in the plot again. I brought up the matter of the exchange of the painting. I said that it would be better to have the exchange of painting and money in Florence, away from local eyes. Then he said "No! We don't trust the Italians, ta' qattani! (They are criminals!). When he calmed down, I returned to the issue of looking after the painting. I am dreading the state that the painting must be in and will have to plan for its restoration.

Tuesday, 7th

Merisi phoned at 8.50 Remind him to take care of the 'St. Jerome' wherever it is. He assures me that the painting is back in Malta.

In the afternoon I went to the Gozo Archaeological Museum. I met the Minister who told me that I should ask M. for proof that the painting was in Malta. He told me that he had a plan in mind, but did not specify.

Thursday, 9th

Opening of Parliament.

M. phoned at 08.40 I told him that I had a committee meeting - could he phone later?

At this time I was expected to go to Russia. Many years before, way back in 1974, I had been one of the founding members of the Maltese Soviet Friendship Society. I had been offered an invitation to Russia at the time - now I was being invited again.

Foundation of the Maltese Soviet Friendship Society in front of Sciortino's Checkov at the Fine Arts Museum - 1974

Dr Roganov from the Russian Embassy came to see me today. He has been phoning me a number of times seeking confirmation that I will go to Russia. I would love to accept but this is a very difficult time to leave Malta. We seem so close to retrieving the painting and yet I am unable to give the main reason why I can not travel. It's a sacrifice, but necessary for however long it takes.

At about 9 p.m. Merisi phoned at the Priory to tell me that he had left a letter in the letterbox. I told him not to use the Priory phone anymore, as everyone would get to know what was going on.

I could imagine a "friendly" busybody having a great time messing things up. Besides, my intention was that Merisi would use the Archaeology Museum telephone which was better equipped to trace the calls.

Tuesday, 14th

Another piece of very good news. One of the telephone technicians tells me that he has actually seen the two men going into a photographer's shop to buy a roll of film. The technician had recognised and followed them. Unfortunately, after following the two men for some distance, he lost sight of them.

I received some photos of the stolen 'St. Jerome' in the post. The painting is photographed next to a copy of yesterday's Times of Malta – this could be proof that the painting is now in Malta.

At a reception at the French Embassy I informed the Minister accordingly. He told me that he had convinced the Prime Minister to get an ex-policeman to help.

I had made this suggestion a long time ago. If it had been accepted then, it would have saved me all those months of agony and worry.

Wednesday, 15th

Received a phone call from M. at about 11 I told him that I was busy. Then he phoned again a while later. We spoke about the photos that they had sent. I told him that they were acceptable to me but might not be to others. There was no postmark on the envelope and the photo of The Times was very blurred. I had handed them over to someone the day before who now had to show them to someone else. They would just have to send clearer photos! I also told them that I had missed out on a trip to Russia because of this lengthy ordeal. Rather subdued, he listened and then said

"Yes, you are right, but we are under pressure here too."

Thursday, 16th

M. called. Told him not to expect a final decision, at least, not just yet. Also told him that the authorities concerned were being consulted and things were now moving nicely.

This ought to give him the idea that a decision is imminent - it is now just a matter of time.

Friday, 17th

Today M. phoned a couple of times but my secretary kept up the charade, saying that I was not available.

Monday, 20th

Phone call from M. at 8.40 As soon as I answered, M. started to complain. I shouted him down – I had done everything possible. I had kept the police out … I had stuck to the price that we had agreed on … I had accepted to have the exchange take place in Malta … I had also missed out on a trip to Russia… I had been put on valium for months. After all I was only the messenger. M. was evidently taken aback and hung up. Then he phoned again and said he would give me till Wednesday. I pretended that I was very angry. I would not accept conditions. He said they would turn to someone else. I told him 'go ahead!'

Later I was amused to hear that someone had picked up a conversation amongst M. and his group. He heard them complain that they were not getting anywhere. He heard them say "Father is laying down his own conditions, instead of accepting ours."

Wednesday, 22nd

M. phoned lots of times today; my secretary told him that I was at the Ministry. I expected that he would phone again and waited to take the call. When he did call, I was gentle with him – told him there were no problems at the moment but that we might need to sort out some details later on.

Later the Minister promised to come to the Museum, but asked me to meet him in his office tomorrow instead.

Thursday, 23rd

The police go marching in!

At 12.30 I met the Minister in his office at Lascaris. I was introduced to a certain Mr. Calleja who had left the Police Force some years previously. I gave him an account of the whole story. He wanted to see the photos that I had received so far and suggested that we should ask for more photographic evidence. We concluded the meeting with the Minister saying to Mr. Calleja, "Make sure you take care of Father Mario." This is something I will never forget.

Saturday, 25th

In the middle of all that is going on I must somehow manage to carry on with the rest of my work – and other activities. Started to paint portrait of Anna Ganado – a dear friend. Am also restoring an old painting belonging to Prof. Lanza.

Monday, 27th

M. phoned at 8.45. In the evening Mr. Calleja came to the Priory to see the Polaroid photographs, the first tape etc. Calleja then asked the date that M. & Co. had been seen on their way to the photographer's shop.

Wednesday, 29th

Got the information that Calleja had asked for yesterday –gave him the details over the phone.

Phone call from M. at 12.45. Told him that everything is going according to plan. Want to maintain the impression that things are reaching a conclusion and that it ought to be over soon.

Thursday, 30th

Another phone call from M. at 11.20. Told him that there was no news yet. He insisted that they wanted to complete the deal within the month. I said, "I hope so too, I have already told you that I need to go abroad!"

Friday, 31st

...Life goes on...

Antiquities Committee meeting. One particular member,

politically involved, throws his weight around and objects to everything I am doing, becoming quite a nuisance in the process. He produced a written request asking me to stop the construction work on the underground Gallery. I took him by surprise when I asked all present to take a vote on this issue. Only one other member supported him and, with a forthcoming art exhibition that I needed to attend to, I just walked out of the meeting.

This evening Mr. Calleja and the telephone technician came over to the Priory.

Mr. Calleja and I worked well together on the case, even though it was for such a short time - not more than a week in fact. It was a pity that I had not been introduced to him earlier.

Monday, 3rd

There was an early phone call this morning soon after I arrived at the office. I passed notes to my secretary - to tell M. that I was at the Central Bank and - No, I would not return early as I had an important meeting with the Prime Minister. It worked! They were suitably impressed.

Mr. Calleja arrived late at the Museum and so missed the phone call. We waited for the rest of the morning in case M. would phone again. Mr. Calleja told me that he had a helicopter and some men standing by.

We waited till 3pm to see if M. would phone. He did not, so we left the Museum.

Chapter 6

DAY OF PROVIDENCE

Tuesday, 4th

Full scale figure of St. Dominic.
By Fr. Zerafa at De Porres Hall Sliema.

St. Dominic's Day

August 4th was the traditional feast day of my holy father, St Dominic.

At the age of 16, I had joined the Dominican Order and lived happily ever after. My going into a monastery had been a surprise to all who knew me, except perhaps to Dun Gorg Preca, who had given me every encouragement. My life had been a very happy one – the best one could desire. I had a loving family, the best of friends, and work that was a labour of love.

The Dominican star had been a great ideal to follow. In this case I felt confident that St. Dominic 'benigno ai suoi e ai nemici crudo' would understand and would not let me down.

He certainly did not!

The phone rang at 8.15 ...

Behind the closed doors of my office in the Museum, Calleja sat next to me at my desk. Whisky was served, washed down with cups of tea.

Cigarette butts filled the ashtray while smoke from my pipe filled the room. It would have made a lovely film.

Calleja had two radios but one had a spent battery.

There was another Mr. Calleja, head of the Armed Forces, a helicopter circling the skies of Malta. It seemed that there were quite a number of cars – communicating with each other, "Zulu 1..., Zulu 2..." racing round the Island.

...I took the second phone call from M. and Co. I told them that everything was just fine and that there was a 'lawyer' next to me with the money – would they like to have a word with him? They said they certainly would. I passed the phone to Calleja who asked them to cut another piece of canvas from the painting and to put it somewhere and then let us know precisely where it was. Once we found this piece of canvas, we would give them the money ...

At 10.47 the old voice I had got to know so well, called to tell me that they 'had put the piece of canvas in [of all places] the Priory letterbox. [In fact they had not.]

I asked Calleja if the Police Force had any sniffer dogs that could pick up the trail from a piece of canvas. He phoned the Police Depot and was told that their dogs were only trained to sniff for drugs. I then asked Calleja if his men knew what they were looking for. He said that he had kept this as top secret to the very end. This meant that his team most probably had little or no idea of what the painting looked like! I sent an urgent message to Dominic to send me 10 postcards of the 'St. Jerome' from the Museum book shop.

The car chase near Castille

All this time, Mr. Calleja was in my office maintaining contact with the other Calleja, who was circling over the factory area in the helicopter. At one time the helicopter pilot informed us that they could see someone leaving the factory. The Mr.Calleja in my office gave orders to the Mr. Calleja in the helicopter to arrest them. I stopped him and said, "No! Not until we know where the painting is." Calleja ordered, "Cancel previous order!" The answer came back "What previous order?" At one point, to my great surprise, Calleja just rushed out of my office without a word...

I came back to the Priory, feeling totally bewildered and very worried. Mr. Calleja had not looked too happy either. I did not know what was on his mind. Naturally I expected to find the piece of canvas that they said they had posted in the letterbox.

The Prior was ill in bed at the time but he told me there had been no mail for me this morning. I felt desperate. We had been promised the delivery of the piece of canvas – which had not materialised. What sort of trick were they playing? I phoned Dominic...nobody had any news.

These were probably the worst hours in all the months of cat and mouse manoeuvring.

At about 3 p.m. there was a loud knocking at the Priory door. This is the time that the fathers at the Priory have their siesta and the loud knocking at the door would be the last thing that they

Suspects being escorted to the Police HQ in Floriana

would welcome. I looked out of my window and asked the man to stop the knocking but he made much more noise by shouting even louder. "WE'VE CAUGHT THEM!!" He was obviously a policeman in civvies. I asked him, "What about the painting?" The policeman just repeated "We've caught them!" I ran down to meet him and he drove me straight to the Police Depot.

At the Depot I found all the people who had been involved in the chase – the men who had been in the helicopter, and in the cars and those who had co-ordinated matters at the Police Station. There was Dr. De Marco, Minister for Police and Dr. Mifsud Bonnici, Minister of Culture. Above all there was 'my' Caravaggio, still only half visible in a roll of synthetic leather, on a table. What a sight for sore eyes! I could see that the painting was badly damaged but it was a miracle that it was there at all. I think that I

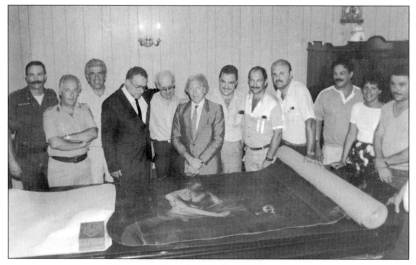

The picture that tells it all. The men involved in the recovery

Congratulated by the P.M.

almost fainted. The police were very generous with their whiskies.

I felt great. The Prime Minister came in and hugged me. I asked for Dominic. I was told he was outside, so I went out and called him in. There were plenty of speeches but no words could express what had happened and what I felt. For so long we had given up all hope of seeing the painting again - now it is back!

The police had earlier changed their motto from 'Domine Dirige nos' to 'Ad populi commoditatem. ' I said to the policemen present, "Isn't it time that you went back to the old motto?"

I told the Minister that I should go over to the Curia opposite the Depot and inform the Archbishop of the recovery. The Minister told me that he would tell the Archbishop himself.

Later on the Archbishop would tell me that nobody had informed him that the missing painting had been recovered.

I never really got to know the details of the last phases of the chase. Nor do I think it all that important. We knew the names of the thieves and had their photos from the workbooks, so apprehending them in Malta was not such an impossible task. In fact, very little was revealed to me – or to the press. I know the helicopter had been following the car since the moment it left the factory. I have seen a photograph of the car being stopped somewhere close to Castille showing the man being apprehended.

Although this information is not first hand, it was said that he was carrying the piece of canvas that he was supposed to have dropped in the Priory letter box and also had a cutting of the Times Of Malta reporting the theft of the painting almost three years before. Apparently he gave up at once and led the police to where the painting was supposed to have been hidden. It seems that at the last moment the other person involved, (Merisi) had moved it to a safer place. At first, it seems, he denied any knowledge of the theft but after he was told that the police had all the necessary evidence, he had to own up.

Recovery of stolen Caravaggio

SIR, – All sorts of fancy stories have been told about the recovery of Caravaggio's *St. Jerome*.

The latest one to come out probably beats all others in its fairness, modesty and strict adherence to facts.

An exhibition of Caravaggio's works was recently held in Florence and later in Rome. An impressive official catalogue came out in Florence and another one with some additional pages added to cover the Rome exhibition.

In the Rome catalogue our *St. Jerome* was included even though it did not feature in the exhibition. In the write-up on the *St. Jerome* a brief account of the theft was given and the story concluded with the following words: *"è stata recuperata il 4 agosto 1987 dai* Carabinieri del Nucleo Recupero Opere d'Arte di Roma." (p. 380)!

"E se non ridi, di che rider suoli?...

Yours truly,
Sliema. · **M.J.Ž.**

The Sunday Times - July 26, 1992

I was quoted later as saying that it had been easier to deal with the Mafia than to work with some of the Ministers and Monsignori. If you are looking for proof of this, well…. just read on. But the Ms & Ms were not the only ones to cause trouble. Later on, some Italians would claim in a very matter of fact manner that it was the Italian police who had recovered the painting! This was not just a case of careless reporting in a popular newspaper either. It was a factual statement in an official publication.

Naturally, this was yet another case of "there's no business like show business".

Since our people in Rome did not know and did not seem to care about the true story, I felt that I had to make the picture clear. I wrote a strong letter to the press.

"E se non ride …"

Interlude

Hard facts… not hard feelings.

Churchill would have described the hour of the recovery of the painting as my finest hour – the ecstasy after the agony. Everyone was happy, well almost everyone. One always gets the occasional spiv out to be a nuisance. One such spiv (Churchill may have had someone like him in mind when he used the term),phoned to congratulate me. I had learnt to humour him so I thanked him profusely. This did not satisfy him. He came all the way to the Priory in Sliema, dragging his poor wife with him. I invited him up to my room as I was waiting to hear the announcement of the recovery of the painting on the eight o'clock news. I was not disappointed. It was the first item of news.

"THE CARAVAGGIO HAS BEEN RECOVERED. TWO MEN ARE BEING HELD BY THE POLICE. A PRIEST IS INVOLVED!!"

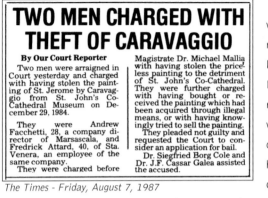

TWO MEN CHARGED WITH THEFT OF CARAVAGGIO

By Our Court Reporter

Two men were arraigned in Court yesterday and charged with having stolen the painting of St. Jerome by Caravaggio from St. John's Co-Cathedral Museum on December 29, 1984.

They were Andrew Facchetti, 28, a company director of Marsascala, and Fredrick Attard, 40, of Sta. Venera, an employee of the same company. They were charged before

Magistrate Dr. Michael Mallia with having stolen the priceless painting to the detriment of St. John's Co-Cathedral. They were further charged with having bought or received the painting which had been acquired through illegal means, or with having knowingly tried to sell the painting.

They pleaded not guilty and requested the Court to consider an application for bail.

Dr. Siegfried Borg Cole and Dr. J.F. Cassar Galea assisted the accused.

The Times - Friday, August 7, 1987

I poured him a whisky. He poured himself many others. That really loosened his tongue. George Bernard Shaw was certainly right when he said that if you want to know a person's character you have to watch him when he is angry - or drunk. Off he went, his tongue wagging, his folie de grandeur getting bigger with each whisky that he downed.

He boasted that he knew where the painting had been because the Italians had told him, "La tila (sic) e' a Malta." I teased him, "Wouldn't the Italians have said "la tela?"

Nothing could stop him now. He turned to Museum matters. He said he was interested in the forthcoming exam for Curator of Fine Arts. I pointed out that the exam was for an assistant Curator. "In that case...," he said "I am not interested." In fact he said that he would go to the Ministry to stop it. He knew that there was someone else who was interested but obviously, in his view, this candidate was not at all suitable. This candidate's involvement in the Caravaggio case would not help him at all. The more whisky he drank, the more names he dropped - all designed to convince me that he had political contacts. To impress me further he said that he had been offered a job at the Ministry. He reminded me that the Minister had defended him legally in the past. He mentioned an MP who he believed had recently spoken to me about him. He was rather taken aback when I told him that I had not had the pleasure to meet this particular MP for over ten years. I offered to phone him up there and then. (He had obviously been taken for a ride.) Incidentally, but not surprisingly, he did not approve of the work I was doing on the new gallery - which probably explained why his party paper had recently spoken of a "Disaster at the museum".

All of this of course, was just 'sound and fury' and it really signified 'nothing' at all. I had got used to him and only felt sorry for him, more so for his family. I had helped him a lot in the past. He had even asked me to tie the knot when he got married. I had encouraged him to study.. as had his aquaintances in Rome; *studia, studia*. And yet he insisted on being a nuisance. To me, to my predecessor and, I understand, to the curator who came after me. He had put all he had in one political basket – this gave him a sense of security but did not add an inch to his stature. I bore him patiently and was willing to forgive him anything…. but spoiling one of my happiest days with his empty talk was a bit too much.

Those familiar with St Jerome's way of writing would accept that he would have expressed himself in much stronger terms. Yet, in spite, or because of his strong character, 'St. Jerome' was a saint.

What was, however, of interest and very worrying in view of what was to happen later, was that he was in possession of information that should never have reached him – whatever his political contacts were.

I do believe that this incident and the unpleasant things that followed should one day be told in full…

Looking back it was well worth the whisky. Probably the moral of all this is that only mature adults should be allowed to drink whisky.

IL SAN GEROLAMO DI
CARAVAGGIO A MALTA

DAL FURTO AL RESTAURO

Extracts from the official report by the Istituto Centrale Del Restauro, Rome

IL RECUPERO

da *Marius Zerafa**

Il 29 dicembre 1985 il dipinto fu asportato dalla sede in cui veniva esposto negli anni più recenti, il museo attiguo alla concattedrale di San Giovanni alla Valletta.

La sera del 24 novembre '86 fu recapitata all'allora Direttore dei Musei di Malta, Marius Zerafa, una busta: dentro c'era una foto del dipinto ed una cassetta registrata, con la quale si chiedeva un riscatto di mezzo milione di sterline maltesi (quasi due miliardi di lire).

La voce maschile inoltre informava che il dipinto era in mani italiane, e se le Autorità non avessero consegnato la somma entro una settimana l'opera sarebbe andata definitivamente perduta.

Dal giorno successivo la stessa voce tornò a farsi sentire per telefono parecchie volte, presentandosi da un certo momento in poi con lo pseudonimo allusivo di "Merisi".   Sollecitava una risposta e, ovviamente, diffidava dall'informare le forze dell'ordine o la stampa.

In realtà sembrò allora più opportuno avvertire in via riservata il Ministro competente e interessare l'italiano Nucleo dei Carabinieri per la tutela del patrimonio artistico, ovviamente in possesso di un'esperienza specifica che le locali forze di polizia non potevano avere.

Fu così che ai primi di dicembre due funzionari del Nucleo si recarono a Malta per concordare il da farsi.   Oltre a consigliare di prendere tempo, suggerirono di cercare di ottenere dai ladri che lo scambio avvenisse in Italia per collaborare alla loro cattura.

Di fronte alle sempre più insistenti sollecitazioni telefoniche del sedicente Merisi, Zerafa chiese di avere una prova tangibile che egli era veramente in grado di garantire la consegna dell'opera.   Gli pervenne una busta contenente una strisciolina di tela dipinta, frammento (gli si assicurava) del *San Gerolamo*.

---

* La dinamica del furto è tuttora in via di ricostruzione da parte di competenti organi della Repubblica di Malta, mentre è possibile ripercorrere qui per sommi capi le vicende del recupero grazie alla cortesia del protagonista di esso Marius Zerafa, che ha messo a nostra disposizione il resoconto di una storia intricata e spesso ai limiti del giallo.

5

* The date 1985 is obviously wrong. It should read '29 Dicembre 1984'.

Pochi giorni dopo, il 12 dicembre, gli giunse una seconda foto del quadro ripreso assieme alla copia di un quotidiano italiano: questa volta erano ben visibili dei danni alla superficie pittorica, soprattutto in corrispondenza del braccio destro del *Santo*.

Subito dopo arrivò, sempre via telefono, il secondo ultimatum. Il fatto però che questa volta si concedessero quindici giorni indusse Zerafa e gli altri che seguivano la vicenda a supporre che il "Merisi" non disponesse di altre concrete alternative.

Zerafa prese pertanto a mercanteggiare sul prezzo, dicendo che lo riteneva troppo alto.

L'ultimo dell'anno i ladri si dichiararono disposti ad accettare l'offerta di 350.000 sterline maltesi, respingendo nel contempo l'ipotesi di effettuare lo scambio in Italia, a Roma o a Firenze.

Da quel momento in poi Zerafa procurò di non essere raggiunto dalle telefonate del "Merisi". La trattativa però non poteva protrarsi troppo a lungo, nonostante la campagna elettorale che, per un certo periodo, aveva costituito un ottimo pretesto per dilazionare l'incontro.

Ad un tratto nel negoziato ci fu una svolta, le telefonate vennero fatte da un'altra voce maschile. Ma, per fortuna, nello stesso tempo cominciarono a dare i primi risultati le intercettazioni alle quali era stato sottoposto il telefono di Zerafa, certi sospetti cominciarono a prendere forma. Quando ci fu la sensazione che non si poteva più ricorrere a pretesti di nessun tipo per guadagnare altro tempo, a otto mesi dalla prima telefonata dei ladri, furono consegnati alla polizia maltese tutti gli elementi di cui si era in possesso, compresi le ipotesi e i sospetti.

Da allora (23 luglio '87) e fino al giorno in cui la vicenda ebbe felice conclusione l'affare fu gestito dalle locali forze dell'ordine, ovviamente in modo professionale: con intercettazioni, pedinamenti, sorveglianza continua su individui sospetti.

Il 4 agosto, su suggerimento degli investigatori, Zerafa fece sapere al suo ancora ignoto interlocutore che aveva con sé i soldi per il riscatto e che era pronto ad effettuare lo scambio, ma prima esigeva la consegna immediata di un'altra striscia di tela del dipinto a riprova che il *San Gerolamo* fosse ancora a Malta.

Poco dopo la polizia riuscì ad arrestare due maltesi che pedinava da tempo, ritrovando in tasca ad uno di essi la strisciolina di tela.

Il dipinto fu, subito dopo, rinvenuto nascosto all'interno di una grossa pelle conciata arrotolata nel calzaturificio di tale Facchetti.

6

Chapter 7

TWISTED BY KNAVES TO MAKE A TRAP FOR FOOLS

Wednesday, 5th

The day after the recovery was a day of celebration.

Many friends and many art lovers, called, wrote or phoned to express their joy and satisfaction. Bottles of whisky went to friends who had helped. Crates of beer and cakes went to the staff. The phone rang constantly. I had to explain to my staff why, for the first time ever, my office door at the Archaeology Museum had been locked all day. Some thought I was having problems with the Minister – they were wrong. Others thought of less unpleasant things – they were wrong too. On the whole everyone was overjoyed. The Minister's son insisted on driving me home this evening.

At the time, my greatest wish was to get back to normality – some would call it my 'normal abnormality'. I asked to have my old telephone number back. A number of cultural events including Maltafest were being organised. That meant that there was a substantial

---

24   THE TIMES, WEDNESDAY, AUGUST 5, 1987

PRIME MINISTER HAILS RECOVERY OF "ST. JEROME" AS 'BRILLIANT OPERATION'

By Our Parliamentary Correspondents

The Prime Minister, Dr. Eddie Fenech Adami, speaking in the House of Representatives yesterday, hailed the recovery of Caravaggio's "St. Jerome" as "a brilliant operation".

In a statement, Dr. FENECH ADAMI said he informed the House of the recovery of the Caravaggio with great pleasure, a pleasure which, he was sure, they shared not only with the people of Malta but also with the rest of the civilized world.

This was the result, Dr. FENECH ADAMI said, of a brilliant operation conducted by the Police led by Supt. Alfred Calleja.

The Caravaggio was stolen in December 1984 and the Police immediately started investigations. Dr. FENECH ADAMI also paid tribute to Dr. Carmelo Mifsud Bonnici, Prime Minister at the time of the theft, who on leaving office had immediately informed the Minister of Culture (Dr. Ugo Mifsud Bonnici) of developments in the investigations up to that stage.

The investigations had continued, Dr. FENECH ADAMI said, and he praised the Director of Museums, Fr. Marius Zerafa, for his interest, forbearance, prudence and good sense which helped the investigations to bear fruit.

The merit for the finding of the Caravaggio certainly belonged to many, including Dr. Carmelo Mifsud Bonnici, former Ministers and Ministers who had given particular attention to the case.

The operation was conducted by Supt. Alfred Calleja, who was helped by Inspectors Angelo Farrugia, Paul Sammut, Charles Galea and Charles Cassar of the Special Mobile Unit, while Col. Maurice Calleja, Commander of the Task Force, and his men, provided support.

The painting was not irreparably damaged and restoration will be carried out, Dr. FENECH ADAMI said. He added that at various stages in the investigation there was help from Interpol and from the Italian Government.

Dr. FENECH ADAMI finally thanked everybody connected with the retrieval of the painting and said he was sure everyone shared in the joy.

SECURITY AT ST. JOHN'S

Mr. RENO CALLEJA (MLP) said the Opposition welcomed the recovery of the stolen Caravaggio. He asked what steps had been taken to tighten security at St. John's Co-Cathedral, and whether talks could be initiated with Church authorities, who had an enormous art treasure in their care, for greater security, especially in these wayside chapels, and to share with Government the costs of such security measures.

Mr. DOM MINTOFF (MLP) asked whether Government agreed that a classification exercise should be undertaken of the various art treasures in Malta, treasures of which some of the churches were not even aware. Should not some international expert be commissioned to carry out a survey?

Dr. FENECH ADAMI said the Government had already taken measures to step up security at St. John's Co-Cathedral. Government planned to draw up an inventory of works of art in its possession, which could also include art works belonging to the Church and to private collections. He agreed that certain works of art in our churches were not fully appreciated, and that it was important to know first what we had, in order to conserve it.

Dr. UGO MIFSUD BONNICI, Minister of Education and Culture, said that Unesco had already been asked to help in the drawing up of an inventory of art works in Malta.

CUMBERSOME PROCEDURES

The House then continued to debate the second reading of the European Convention Bill.

Dr. JOSEPH BRINCAT (MLP), resuming his speech from Monday's sitting, said Clause 4 of the bill, regarding procedures to be followed in human rights cases, was taken word for word from the old Section 47 of the Constitution. These procedures were cumbersome and time-wasting; it is true that they had to start within eight days, but they could drag on and on. This very week the First Hall of the Civil Court decided on a case started more than four years ago.

The procedure was cumbersome because the First Hall of the Civil Court had to stop hearing its other cases in order to deal with Constitutional cases, no matter how frivolous.

Dr. BRINCAT said he felt the rules of procedure should be changed. He was sure that even the Judges of first instance were fed up with them. The First Hall should be bypassed completely, because in any case its decision would be appealed.

Dr. BRINCAT said that the claim, and the counter-claim, should be substantiated by affidavit. This would then go directly to the Constitutional Court.

Dr. BRINCAT said that the Constitution already safeguarded human rights, which were after all principles of natural justice which should be applied by any Court. In this bill, Malta was adhering to a declaration of principles which had to be safeguarded in any case. It was Malta's second Bill of Rights.

As for the enforceability of the decisions of the European Court of Human Rights, this could have been obtained simply by amending the Interpretation Act in the sense that no law can be interpreted in such a way as to go against the human rights principles.

The system needed overhauling, as it led to duplication of effort and certain procedures needed a radical rethinking. Dr. BRINCAT suggested that one of the Judges could collect the evidence relating to an alleged human rights abuse; once the evidence is collected he would then sit with two other Judges in order to give a collegial decision.

Dr. BRINCAT described as illogical the procedure whereby, after accepting the compulsory jurisdiction of the European Court, its decisions cannot be made enforceable except through the decision of a Lower (Maltese) Court.

Dr. BRINCAT said the bill, as drafted, would needlessly complicate matters in Malta and in Strasbourg. He urged the collection of evidence by affidavit first, after which the case would go to the Constitutional Court or to the Court of Appeal. According to the bill, although the Constitutional Court is Malta's Supreme Court, the Appeal Court would be in a position to change a decision by the Constitutional Court.

As for reservations on human rights as drawn up in the bill, Dr. BRINCAT said that the only exclusions allowed were those which Malta made when adhering to the Convention in 1966.

Dr. BRINCAT said that the bill should be studied carefully, especially in the committee stage, because of its repercussions on other laws and the reflection it cast on the Constitution.

Dr. JOSEPH FENECH Parliamentary Secretary for Maritime Affairs said that the Opposition was attacking the modalities of the bill and bringing arguments of convenience, although the points raised by the Leader of the Opposition were valid.

Dr. FENECH said the bill made the European Convention an integral part of Maltese law and also provided for decisions given by the European Court of Human Rights enforceable also in Malta.

He referred to a suggestion made by Dr. Brincat regarding the procedure of affidavit. Experience showed that this procedure was useless and sometimes only served to make proceedings even longer.

He said Dr. Brincat had also stated that the bill was in conflict with certain parts of the Constitution. The Constitution had certain reservations and the bill was now eliminating them, Dr. FENECH said.

IN THE EUROPEAN MAINSTREAM

Dr. MICHAEL FRENDO (PN) said that in March 1946 the German Christian Democratic Party had declared that society and the citizen was more important than the State. It was the State which protected the citizen and not vice-versa, the German party had declared.

It was in this light that the bill should be seen. This Government was not a miser where fundamental human rights were involved, Dr. FRENDO said.

He said the bill did not make any reservations and so it applied to every sector of the legal system.

Dr. FRENDO said it was the people who had won their fundamental human rights under a Socialist Government. Take people like Salvu Gauci, Carmel Cacopardo, and Censu Galea among many others, he said. The Socialist Government had a record of human rights violations.

The bill was a process that put the country in the mainstream of European civilization, Dr. FRENDO said. It was a bill which continued to prepare the country towards full membership with the European Community. It also gave the country the image it deserved, the image of a serious country cherishing fundamental human rights and where the rule of law was always upheld.

He said the bill formed part of the crusade for the rights of the Maltese people, a crusade which the Government embarked upon as soon as it was elected to power.

It was shameful for the Socialist Government which for 16 years failed to recognize the right to individual petition only to give this right in its last days in power.

Dr. FRENDO said the previous Government had decided to grant this right as it thought others would act in the same way it had.

Mr. JOSEPH SCIBERRAS (MLP) said Dr. Frendo had mentioned certain names but failed to say that this Government had denied work to employees of the Foreign Office because of "exigencies of service". He said he doubted whether there was any need for the bill once the persons mentioned by Dr. Frendo had sought redress and won their case.

Mr. SCIBERRAS said he had served the previous Government at the Council of Europe and therefore he was very familiar with the procedures that had to be followed for a case to be taken to the Council and how long it would take.

He said he was interested in how the bill affected the ordinary citizen. The ordinary citizen would first spend large sums of money to hire a lawyer to take his case to the first and second Court in Malta. Then he would need more money to keep the case going at the European Court for so many years.

The Labour MP said the bill lacked a clause providing for Government financial assistance to those wanting to take their claim to Strasbourg. Without such a clause the bill was useless as no ordinary citizen could afford it, unless the case was not referred to Strasbourg by an association. Mr. SCIBERRAS said no political party should think of using the Convention for political ends as by the time the case was decided by the European Court the legislature would come to an end and a new one elected.

Mr. SCIBERRAS said he felt that either in the bill or elsewhere provisions should be made for financial assistance if the ordinary citizen was to benefit from the proposed measure.

*   *   *

The rest of the debate will be reported tomorrow. The House yesterday rose at 9.30 p.m. and adjourned till today at 6 p.m.

CARAVAGGIO RECOVERED

amount of work for our department to deal with. I was Director of Museums working from my office in the Museum of Archaeology, but for many years the Department had no Curator of Fine Arts. So I had to take care of any matters that concerned the Fine Arts, as well as those of other museums.

The Arts have always been my prime interest, so any work to do with the Arts was, for me, a labour of love – but it was still hard work.

At the opening of an exhibition, I spoke of my idea a new project for a decent exhibition hall. This had been a life long dream of mine. I read out a letter that I had written to the Times of Malta many years before, when the National Museum had first been inaugurated.

Back then, I did not have the faintest idea that I would one day form part of the Museums Department. At the time of writing the letter to the Times of Malta I was studying in Florence. With the help and encouragement of Giorgio La Pira, who had been the Mayor of Florence as well as a Dominican Tertiary and a very good friend, I was planning to open an art centre in San Marco in Florence and settle there for good. I had enrolled at the University to read for a doctorate in Art History and had already finished all the exams.

Leaving Florence and coming back to Malta is one of a very few regrets that I have in life.

In my letter to The Times I remember that I had congratulated all concerned for a job well done but had also appealed for a new hall for contemporary exhibitions.

I felt that a Museum Curator would not be doing his job merely by preserving relics from the past. I also believed that all promising contemporary artists deserved encouragement and opportunity. I had kept in mind what Pope John XXIII had once said to us when I was a student of Social Sciences and Art History in Rome, "You have come into this world not to look after a Museum but to look after a garden!"

As for the 'St. Jerome' – it was crying out for restoration. The painting just lay in a box at the Police Depot, the canvas still unstretched. Much of the pigment, particularly in the highlights, had become detached from the canvas. We had prepared a special box for the painting. The top priority now, was to get the painting relined and stretched at once. I was sure that the Italian Government – who had been so quick to help with the first restoration in the 1950s – would now provide transport and all the assistance necessary to have it restored again.

I was hoping, too, that we had learnt our lesson and that now serious security would be drawn up for St. John's as well as Malta's other museums. I discussed this at length with the Minister. I put before him the numerous problems we had at the Museum and which I sincerely hoped would eventually be resolved.

"St. Jerome" at the Istituto di Restauro -still unrestored!

Welcome back, St. Jerome

● All Maltese of good taste (and good will) were overjoyed to learn that the probe started by former Premier Karmenu Mifsud Bonnici into the robbery of Caravaggio's **St Jerome** was crowned with success when the priceless painting was recovered after nearly three years. **St Jerome** dates back to the early 1600s when Caravaggio was commissioned to carry out work for St John's in Valletta and is considered to be one of his masterpieces. It shows St Jerome, naked to the waist, sitting on a couch, engaged in one of his writings. The model is thought to be Grand Master Alof de Wignacourt; indeed the resemblance is striking. With the return of St Jerome the Maltese can sigh with relief and resolve to take greater care of their art treasures.

Chronicle - Saturday, August 8, 1987

Saturday, 15th

A reception at the Italian Embassy. I asked the Italian Ambassador to help. He was very friendly and expressed his appreciation for what I had done in connection with the 'St. Jerome'. He also said that someone had told him that years before I had been recommended for an Italian award by Ambassador Giglioli, but this had been 'bloccata' by a previous government. I had also heard the same story from Prof. Dorigo who had told me that the reason was probably because someone else had been nominated. My Minister was following the conversation and, with his usual enthusiasm said, 'Sblocchiamola!' I always admired his command of words.

Later the French Government would award me the far more prestigious Chevalier des Arts et des Lettres. At the Quattorze Juillet ceremony, on presentation of the medal, the French Ambassador spoke of the recovery of the 'St. Jerome'.

It was quite amusing to hear a friend saying, Quod non fecerunt...

Tales and rumours of the theft and recovery of the 'St. Jerome' painting abounded. At a reception a Minister who had been a good friend of mine since childhood, recounted how one Monsignor told him that the theft had been commissioned by, of all people, President Bourguiba! [Former President of Tunisia]. This Monsignor had sought a meeting with the Prime Minister and had also tried his story on other Ministers.

The '*St. Jerome*' episode was recounted in various newspapers, local as well as foreign. A dramatic account of the Caravaggio theft and recovery appeared in the Italian magazine, Epoca. Friends were good enough to send me cuttings of this and other foreign papers that reported the recovery.

Chevalier des Art set des Lettres

Monday, 31st

Mr. Calleja came to the Priory and we discussed the court case. Almost as an aside, he told me that I had been close to being the first person ever to be kidnapped in Malta. Apparently the thieves had commissioned a man from Santa Lucia to kidnap me during the exchange in case we tried to fool them. It seems I was worth... LM5,000! I thought he was joking, and said, "That would have livened things up." I was assured that it was no laughing matter – the potential kidnapper was known to be dangerous and dealt in arms and drugs.

When I mentioned the kidnapping at the Priory I was cheerfully told by my one of my brethren that he would have willingly paid an extra LM100 to the kidnappers to keep me...

Police hold three for questioning on Caravaggio

By a Staff Reporter

Three people were yesterday helping the Police in their investigations connected with the theft of the Caravaggio painting "St. Jerome" informed sources said.

The canvas was recovered by the Police on Tuesday, almost three years after it went missing from St. John's Co-Cathedral museum in Valetta.

A wall of official secrecy surrounds the investigations currently going on, led by Superintendent Alfred Calleja. Details of where, how and what led to the recovery of this priceless painting have not been revealed so far. It is known, however, that the painting was found in a factory at Marsa.

The "St. Jerome" is being held under lock and key at the Police Depot in Floriana as it will have to be exhibited in Court if anyone is arraigned in connexion with its theft, the sources said.

The painting depicts St. Jerome, naked to the waist, sitting on a couch and writing. St. Jerome was the translator of the Bible into Latin. It measures 117cm by 157cm and is believed to have been painted by using Grand Master Alof de Wignacourt as a model. The "St. Jerome" was painted for the Chapel of St. Catherine of the Langue of Italy in St. John's and is one of the two Caravaggios in Malta. The other one depicts the beheading of St. John and hangs in the Oratory of St. John's Co-Cathedral.

HOME-MADE I ON MARSA R(

By a Staff Reporter

The Task Force explosive ordnance disposal unit yesterday morning rendered safe a medium-sized home-made bomb found by a street-cleaner at Triq il-Hazna, which leads from Belt il-Hazna to the Menqa, in Marsa.

The bomb, contained in a small Farleys tin with two fuses sticking out, was found at 8.10 a.m. by a cleaner in the grass on a roundabout. It was for some reason carried across the road onto a pavement and the Task Force was then alerted.

The road was closed to traffic and the Task Force men, who were led by Major Albert Camilleri, carried the bomb to a safer area on the other side of the roundabout where it was found

The Times - Thursday, August 6, 1997

ERA STATO RUBATO NEL 1984

Recuperato dalla polizia maltese il «San Gerolamo» del Caravaggio

LA VALLETTA — La polizia maltese ha ritrovato il «San Gerolamo» del Caravaggio rubato dal museo della cattedrale di S. Giovanni, alla Valletta, il 29 dicembre 1984.

Parlando ieri pomeriggio al quartier generale della polizia, dove il quadro era stato riportato appena due ore prima, il ministro dell'interno Guido De Marco ha elogiato la polizia maltese «che ha concluso questa brillante opera di recupero senza alcun aiuto straniero. Ha dichiarato De Marco: «questa certamente ridarà alla polizia maltese la stima che merita.

Il quadro fu eseguito nel 1608 e, secondo gli esperti, aveva posato per l'artista lo stesso gran maestro dell'ordine di S. Giovanni, Alof De Wignacourt. Il quadro ha subito danni «molto leggeri», secondo il direttore del museo di Malta, il reverendo Mario Zerafa.

Secondo Alfred Calleja, il commissario di polizia che ha diretto le inda[...] solo due giorni fa, ma [...] già da qualche setti[...] alcuni arresti, ma c[...] particolari, neanche [...] to il quadro.

«Il successo dell'[...] sorpresa e alla ma[...] Calleja, ha definito il [...] nici, ha definito il ra[...] ravaggio come «un[...] Malta ma per il m[...]

Il «San Gerolamo[...] una mostra dedi[...] tese, ha aggiunto [...] un altro Caravag[...] vanni», considera[...] lavoro, esposto n[...] (Ansa)

Malta, un imputato: "Il mandante è un conte"

Per il furto di un Caravaggio accusati anche tre italiani

LA VALLETTA — Sarebbero stati tre italiani gli autori materiali del clamoroso furto del «San Gerolamo» di Caravaggio, avvenuto il 30 dicembre 1984 dal museo della cattedrale di S. Giovanni alla Valletta. Lo ha dichiarato nella sua testimonianza alla polizia, resa pubblica ieri al processo in corso nella capitale maltese, il ventottenne Andrea Facchetti, figlio del titolare di un calzaturificio a Malta, accusato, insieme a suo cugino Frederick Attard, del furto e della ricettazione del famoso dipinto, ritrovato dalla polizia il 4 agosto scorso.

Facchetti ha affermato che circa 18 mesi fa, mentre stava visitando il museo del Louvre di Parigi insieme al cugino, incontrò un italiano chiamato Vincenzo, che già conosceva, il quale si rivelò loro come l'autore del furto del Caravaggio, dicendo che gli occorreva il loro aiuto per sbarazzarsi del quadro per la cifra di 500.000 lire maltesi (quasi 2 miliardi di lire). Pochi mesi dopo Facchetti avrebbe di nuovo incontrato Vincenzo a Firenze, dove l'italiano nascondeva il quadro. I responsabili del furto si misero quindi in contatto — promettendo di restituire il «San Gerolamo» in cambio del pagamento del riscatto — con il direttore del museo di Stato di Malta, padre Mario Zerafa. Quel tale Vincenzo, accompagnato da un altro italiano di nome Esposito, portò il quadro nella casa di Attard.

Secondo la testimonianza di Facchetti, il mandante del furto sarebbe stato «un certo conte Orsini che vive a Firenze».

Ritrovato il «Caravaggio»

Il «San Girolamo» del Caravaggio trafugato dalla Co[...]

Il San Girolamo di Michelangelo da Cara[...] Museo della Concattedrale della Valletta nel po[...] cembre 1984 è stato ritrovato. Ne ha dato co[...] al Direttore di questo periodico il Prof. P. Emil[...] dei Musei Statali di Malta. Nessun furto su c[...] è ipotizzato per quattro anni ma semplicemente [...] sa di sprovveduti (per fortuna ladruncoli locali [...]

Il dipinto avrà bisogno di un notevole [...] quanto gravemente danneggiato sia perché, [...] momento del furto, vi è rimasto arrotolato in [...] via perché dalla tela fu tagliato un piccolo [...] tori (cittadini maltesi arrestati) inviarono dur[...] con le Autorità maltesi per fornire prova di [...] tivo, fallace, di conseguire un illecito pagam[...]

San Girolamo fu un tema piuttosto po[...] perché il santo, che aveva difeso la Chiesa [...] eresie dell'epoca, era tornato di attualità ne[...] in seguito al dilagare della Riforma Protes[...] settentrionale. Caravaggio ne eseguì più d'[...] maltese — eseguito su commissione di fr[...] reggeva il Priorato dell'Ordine Gerosolim[...] nuto il migliore, è drammatico. Il Sa[...] asceta assorto nella meditazione della mor[...] dal tavolo) ma anche impegnato nella difesa d[...] tanto il volto e le braccia rivelano un colorito della pelle e conse-[...] scuro di quello del torso, come per lunga esposizione al sole e conse-[...] guente abbronzatura (l'osservazione è di John Cauchi). In fondo [...] a destra, in verticale separazione, si vede lo stemma dei Malaspina.

il-ħajja

tirrispetta l-intelliġenza tieghek

L-Erbgħa, 5 ta' Awissu, 1987   Nru 3,658 — 4ċ

ID-DIĊENZA PUBBLIKA

(Ara editorjal paġna 6)

INSTABET IL-PITTURA TAL-CARAVAGGIO

Il-pittura imprezzabbli tal-Caravaggio il furi tal San Girolamo qed jkteb u jingara mill-Mużew tal-Kon Kattidral ta' San Gwann f'Diċembru, 1984 instabet mill-Pulizija ta' Malta.

Il-Pulizija ma tawx taghrif dwar kif u fejn instabet il-pittura għalkes għadhom qed biss jinvestigaw fuq xi persuni li qed jinnomaw proprju biex jghinu fl-istharrig.

Fl-istess waqt li għamel tal-ġurnata l-Pulizija tal-biċraft, Dr. Eddie Fenech Adami, Prim Ministru, qal li kien ġie infurmat mil-Membri tal-Kunsill u għall-paġa Malti, mod infurmat b'mod li ssibet imressaq tal-pittura Caravaggio f'Diċembru 1984 instigata mil-Mużew tal-Kon Kattidral ta' San Gwann.

Il-Prim Ministru kompl[...] ta kliefu li kif il-Gvern Naz[...] zjonalista dahhal [...] s-xoghom[...] jeħtieġ ma' snizks Lotthar [...] til dwar fejn kienu min[...]

Friday, 4th

In Court.

Am asked to identify the painting as a Caravaggio but then I could not do so since I was involved in the case. I was asked to recommend someone else. Naturally I suggested Dominic Cutajar. Again there was an objection: Mr. Cutajar had also been involved. Finally I suggested Dr. Cauchi, who had been Curator before me.

I was asked a number of questions about the young man who brought the tape and so on.

Friday, 11th

I attended a reception for Gen. Osnato [from the Italian Embassy] at Palazzo Parisio. He and his family were very good to me and he had given us very practical help with the recovery of the painting. I gave him a framed photo of the 'St. Jerome', as I had given Mr. Calleja, with my sincere thanks. The Italian Ambassador was present and he assured me that the restoration was being taken care of - I should jolly well hope so!

Monday, 14th

An old house of character being knocked down. I report to Ministry. I was told to go and stop demolition. Take police officer with me. Surprise! Owner tells me permission to demolish house had already been granted. Antiquities Committee threatens to resign en masse.

The Maltese forensic expert phoned me to discuss the pieces of canvas that had been cut off by the thieves. In return I insisted that he should treat the remaining canvas (the 'St. Jerome'), which was now at the police headquarters, with great care. I reminded him that as the painting was still un-stretched, it was highly susceptible to further damage.

GĦOTJA B'APPREZZAMENT GĦAS-SEJBA TAL-CARAVAGGIO

•FIX-XAHAR ta' Settembru 1987, is-Sur Charles Vassallo, Konslu Ġenerali ta' Malta f'San Francisco, California, ippreżenta lill-Ministru ta' l-Intern, Dr Guido Demarco LL.D. 500 dollaru Amerikan biex dan jgħaddihom lil Commanding Officer tal-Pulizija, il-Kurunell John Spiteri, biex jintużaw mill-fond tal-Pulizija. Din il-preżentazzjoni saret fil-Police Headquarters, fl-Uffiċju tal-Ministru stess, li għaliha attendew fost oħrajn il-Commanding Officer il-Kurunell John Spiteri, id-Deputat Kummissarju Anthony Mifsud Tomasi, l-Assistent Kummissarju tal-Pulizija Paul Attard, is-Suprintendenti Nikol Cutajar, Alfred Calleja, George Grech, Joseph Psaila u l-Ispettur Angelo Farrugia.

Is-Sur Vassallo qal li hu xtaq juri l-apprezzament għax-xogħol li għamlu l-Pulizija ta' Malta fl-investi-gazzjonijiet b'suċċess fis-sejba tal-pittura imprezzabbli tal-Caravaggio. Hu żied jgħid li ġietu din l-idea ta' donazzjoni wara li ltaqa' ma' l-Ispettur Farrugia waqt il-festa ta' Santa Marija ġewwa l-Mosta f'Awissu li għadda.

Fir-ritratt is-Sur Vassallo jidher ma' l-Ispettur Farrugia mal-pittura tal-Caravaggio.

Unfortunately, the painting was taken out of the box, held up as a trophy and photographed a number of times to be reproduced in books. *Photographs taken before and after it was kept at the Depot clearly illustrate how irresponsible it had been to handle the painting in such a manner.*

further the Museum's financial standing.

3. Fr. Zerafa suggested that a request for the installation of a closed-circuit monit service be made to coincide with a similar service for some Government museum The curator added that he expected the existing alarm-system to be connected with the Police H.Q. in the near future.

4. The chairman then remarked that the Reverend chapter had not been informed regarding the recovery of the "St Jerome" and that it would have been a nice gesture had the Vicar General been included in the photograph circulated to the Press. Fr. Zerafa protested that he had not expected the Rev. chapter to thank him for risking his life, but he did expect those responsible to show some interest in the state of the picture. He had kept the Archbishop informed throughout the operation and as soon as the painting had passed into the hands of the Police, he had drawn the attention of the Minister of Education that the Archbishop be informed The Minister undertook to do so immediately and personally. Once the head of the Diocese was informed, Fr. Zerafa felt there was no need to inform anyone else as the news media had flashed it instantly and thus become common knowledge. The photograph carried by the Press included only the people actually involved in the picture's recovery.

5. After the secretary had read a letter from Perfecta Advertising Limited giving quotations for the reproduction of post-cards, it was agreed to allow the project to go on, while the chairman and Mgr. Cassar undertook to explain matters to the Reverend chapter.

6. The meeting was then adjourned for 10 November 1987.

Cutajar
9·XII·1987.

e se non piange...

Friday, 18th

Receive a phone call from an angry Monsignor complaining that he had not been kept informed about the Caravaggio. For some strange reason he believed that I should have informed <u>him</u>, and not the Archbishop of what was going on. He told me that I would have been "given a present" had I informed him accordingly. This was so unbelievable that I motioned to two of my restorers to listen in!

Then, at a St. John Committee meeting I was told 'It would have been nice to include a Monsignor in the photo taken immediately after the recovery of the painting.' E se non piange?

These were not isolated incidents. Some time earlier the Public Works Department had sent a man to be given employment at the museum. He said that his job would be to wind up the clock at St. John's. I explained to him that we could not afford an extra member of staff and in any case, the sacristan at St. John's Co Cathedral could easily manage to see to the clock.

I phoned the Minister to let him know what had happened and he approved wholeheartedly of what I had done. I still remember his very words, "*Ma nhalluhomx jitmelhu bina.*"[*Let's not allow them to take us for a ride!*]

I was therefore very disappointed when a Reverend Monsignor told me that he had also complained of this incident to the very same Minister, who had merely professed ignorance about the whole affair.

I just had no time for these stupid antics with all the other things that I had to worry about. I was chairman of a number of advisory committees – all painfully aware that they were often mere screens for a multitude of unpleasant things.

Sunday, 11 th

Report in The Times of Malta on telephone tapping.

I insist on correction of the title "CURATOR AUTHORIZES PHONE TAPPING" - I had no need, nor power to authorise phone tapping.

It was duly corrected.

LETTERS TO THE EDITOR

STOLEN CARAVAGGIO

From Fr. Marius Zerafa O.P.

Sir, – Please refer to the report under the title "Ex-museums curator had requested phone tapping to trace stolen Caravaggio" (May 11).

While the report itself was fairly acceptable to me, the title, in bold print, was not. It did not correspond to the contents of the report. I appreciate that a correction was published but I still think a number of points should be made absolutely clear to avoid any misunderstanding.

What I stated in court, and this can be checked with the official records, was more or less the following:

Following the delivery of the first tape asking for half a million *liri*, and the first phone calls way back in November 1986, I had, on December 3, asked the minister responsible for telecommunications to have my phone at the Museums Department put under control. This, I was assured, was perfectly legal, and had been done on numerous occasions in the case of threatening calls. *Nobody can ever refer to this as phone tapping.* My purpose was simply to trace where the calls were coming from and recover the painting, not to have any private conversation tapped. There was no need for this as I was the unwilling recipient of these calls and did not need anyone to record what was being said to me. These phone calls continued for eight long months, and very unpleasant they were.

Various methods were used to try to trace the calls but with little success. We did, however, manage on December 31, 1986, to trace a call to the Żejtun area, and later, more specifically to a hotel in Marsascala.

It was in June 1987 that a call was traced to a small factory in Marsa. I went personally to have a look at this factory on June 5 accompanied by a person who unwittingly provided me with some interesting information on the people working there.

On June 18, I asked to have a look at the workbooks of those employed at the factory. These I obtained on June 23, and certain details in them, plus a couple of lucky coincidences at the time, confirmed our suspicions as to the persons who were making the phone calls. All this happened before the month of July 1987.

On July 23, 1987, I contacted the police for the first-time. I was introduced to Mr. A. Calleja (now

Commissioner of Police) by the Minister of Education and after that we worked very closely and very happily together until the painting was finally retrieved on August 4.

One day the whole story will come out. For the moment all I want to say is that, so far as I am concerned, any form of phone tapping was hardly necessary or relevant, and I want to make it absolutely clear that I *never* requested any phone tapping.

Yours truly,
(Fr.) M. ZERAFA,
Sliema.

SCHOOL PREMISES

From Ms Mary Ann Busuttil

Sir, – I would like, to publicly commend the Principal and staff of St. Catherine's School, Sliema, for the hard work they have been through in order to make possible another prize-giving ceremony which was held on April 20.

Everybody present, including the Parliamentary Secretary for Youth and Culture, Dr. Michael Frendo appreciated the fact that the school is giving a great contribution towards education. The dedication of the principal and teachers shows itself in the happy faces of the students – who range from the age of four years to 16.

In view of all this, why then is the government taking so long to move a resolution in Parliament giving the go-ahead to the school to build much needed premises at St. Andrew's?

I implore whoever is responsible to do what has to be done immediately because St. Catherine's School deserves all the support possible. We parents are proud that our children attend this school and we do not want to be let down as the future of our children is very dear to us.

Yours truly,
M. BUSUTTIL,
Birkirkara.

BOYCOTT OF ISRAEL

From Mr. A. Charles

Sir, – Does Malta form part of the Damascus-based Arab League Boycott of Israel Office (May 7)?

Why are Israeli products boycotted only in European Malta? I do miss the excellent Jaffa oranges and other fruits from Israel which are freely available all over Europe.

Yours truly,

The Times - Saturday, May 18, 1991

Friday, 23rd

Leave for London at noon.

At the time there was talk – but only talk – of a big exhibition at the Royal Academy in London: '5000 Years of Maltese Culture'. The title was grandiose enough and the exhibition was meant to cover the period from Prehistory to the award of the George Cross to Malta after World War II.

Incidentally, a big exhibition "The XIII Council of Europe Exhibition" had been held in Malta in the 1960s. It had been a huge success. Exhibits had come from all over Europe. It had as its topic the "Knights of Malta" and had paid tribute to the artists Caravaggio, Preti and Favray. Unfortunately, in spite of committees and a lot of talk, nothing on that scale has ever been done since.

I offered to help with the proposed exhibition in London. One of the first things I was told was that Caravaggio's '*Beheading*' had to be the main attraction. When I argued that we could not deprive Malta of its greatest treasure and that, in any case, it was definitely not in any condition to travel, I suddenly became very unpopular. I was asked to promise not to oppose it. Naturally I refused. I was told in no uncertain terms – '*No Caravaggio- No exhibition!*' Ultimately the whole plan dissolved into air – into thin air!!

Some time later, experts from the Royal Academy came to Malta and confirmed in the Minister's presence that it would have been criminal to move the '*The Beheading*' - I was not just being a spoilsport after all!

Wednesday, 11th

I had to go to court and again give my account of what happened re. 'St. Jerome' etc. I was asked to state when I was told about the call from the hotel. Naturally I had all the details in my diary, but I had been advised not to be too specific. The lawyer quoted an article in an Italian magazine, Epoca, which mentioned phone tapping. I said, you cannot take that article seriously – it had also said my hair stood on end every time the phone rang! (I certainly do not have a huge amount of hair.) He wanted to know the names of everyone involved. I said we only used nicknames. Mr. Calleja, for instance, was 'Kugin' (Cousin).

At that time one political party was accusing the other party of phone tapping. Later on, the parties switched sides. The accusers became the accused. It was typical politics - the pot calling the kettle black.

Phone tapping 'allowed to recover painting'

Steve Chetcuti

BOTH NATIONALIST and Labour governments had allowed the phone recording of the museum director in order to recover a Caravaggio painting, the Prime Minister told a court yesterday.

While testifying in the constitutional case filed by the lawyer of Frederick Attard, who is being charged with the theft of the St Jerome which was painted by Caravaggio, Prime Minister Eddie Fenech Adami said he was informed the recording was authorised by Karmenu Mifsud Bonnici's government.

He said the PN rose to power in 1987 and he authorised the police to maintain the arrangement brokered by the former Labour government in order to help the investigations.

"We had sanctioned the recordings to continue between the museums director, Fr Marius Zerafa, and the people who stole the paintings although he (Fr Zerafa) was not supposed to make any deals," the PM said.

He said the reason behind the decision was so the call could be traced and the perpetrators caught, which is in fact what happened.

The accused, Attard, 51, from Santa Venera, was undergoing criminal proceeding with Andrea Facchetti in 1990 but the case was suspended after his defence lawyer filed a constitutional application asking for the tapes to be exhibited in court as evidence.

The lawyer, Joe Galea Debono, claimed in the application that the phone recordings between the accused were in breach of the latter's constitutional rights.

Furthermore, Dr Galea Debono said the confession made by Attard had to be considered as involuntary because it had been obtained after being confronted with the tapes.

He alleged that the police were very careful not to exhibit the tapes because it would have caused a scandal if it transpired that these tapping techniques were used.

The lawyer said even though the tapes might help the case of the prosecution, this evidence was 'tainted' and was only used to extract a confession from his client.

In the application, Dr Galea Debono asked the court to uphold his client's request to hear all the witnesses necessary in order to prove that the admission was not done voluntarily.

Attard's co-accused, Facchetti, died of a drug overdose at his factory in Marsa in June 1993.

Apart from the theft of the priceless painting on 29 December 1984, the two were accused of receiving stolen goods and with attempting to sell the painting.

During yesterday's proceedings, the Prime Minister testified that a few weeks after the Nationalist victory at the polls in 1987, he was informed by the then education minister, Ugo Mifsud Bonnici, whose portfolio included museums, about the phone tapping by Fr Zerafa.

He said the recordings regarded the St Jerome thefts and the arrangement had been authorised by the former government.

Dr Fenech Adami told the court that Fr Zerafa wanted to know what direction the new government was taking and we, Dr

Mifsud Bonnici and myself, told him to continue with the contacts.

However, he said he was unaware of the passage of the tapes from the authorities before the 1987 election and the authorities after and claimed never to have spoken directly to Fr Zerafa.

The PM said he appointed Alfred Calleja, who rejoined the Corp. after the election victory and went on to become commissioner, to conduct the investigations and the case was solved.

Meanwhile, Dr Galea Debono asked the court to hear the testimony of former commissioner Calleja to try to establish how the tapes changes hands between one administration and another.

But assistant attorney general, Peter Gauchi, objected on the grounds that the evidence requested by counsel was already deemed inadmissible by the court in a hearing in June 1994.

Dr Grech and Dr Donatella Frendo Dimech appeared for the Republic while Dr Galea Debono assisted Attard.

The Malta Indipendent - Thursday, January 21, 1999

Tuesday, 2nd

I had a strange phone call from the Ministry.

Someone from the Ministry was on the phone asking me to go to Paris. At first I thought this was a way of showing appreciation for what I had done to get the painting back. I said that I was busy with other things. The instruction was repeated - 'The Minister wants you to go to Paris.' (There are many temptations that I can resist. An offer to go to Paris is hardly one of them! I gave in.)

I could not understand it then. I am not sure I understand it now. Well, maybe I do. My successor told me that he had a similar experience when he had objected to a precious museum item being sent abroad for an exhibition.

I have been taught that giving in to temptations is something that one eventually regrets. I must confess that this is certainly one I do regret.

Monday, 15th

Returned from Paris.

The reason why I was sent is starting to make sense. My assistant is very worried. While I was away, he was Acting Director for Museums; and he just could not understand the strange things that were happening in connection with the exam for an Assistant Art Curator for the Fine Arts Museum.

My assistant, the Curator of Archaeology, Tancred Gouder, with whom I had worked for so many years and whom I trusted implicitly, was concerned about the way the exam for new assistant curators was being planned.

He insisted that I should go with him to the Examination Branch because he had been told so many things that just did not make sense to him. It seemed as if the old rules no longer applied and new rules had suddenly been thought up. But the eerie thing was that everything to do with the exams seemed to have been arranged the week I was away. To add insult to injury, whenever I pointed out some of the atrocious developments, I was told that the Board could not consult me because I had been abroad!!

The speed with which everything had been 'fixed' was impressive. I'm sure that no Government department has ever worked that fast before! Things did not just happen – they had not evolved, I felt they must have been planned. In the case of the theft of the 'St. Jerome' we were dealing with a Mafia. I felt there was a more subtle Mafia at work here.

Everything my little man had told me the day we found the Caravaggio was starting to make sense. Was it a case of the tail wagging the dog...?

Friday – 11th

The official account of cultural list of achievements of the Ministry for the year came out. First on the list is the new date for Carnival, last is the return of the Caravaggio! King Carnival before Saint Jerome! Poor Saint Jerome!

V   KULTURA

(a) Karnival: rega' nghata l-post propju tieghu qabel ir-Randan.

(b) Zdiedu l-Kuncerti ta' l-Orkestra tat-Teatru Manoel f'San Gwann u postijiet ohra. Ghall-ewwel darba sar Kuncert fl-Ewwel tas-Sena fil-Palazz Presidenzjali, u Kuncert ta' Muzika Sagra fil-Kolleggjata ta' Bormla, Kuncert ta' Muzika miktuba minn Carlo u Frankie Diacono u ta' Maestro Paolo Nani.

(c) Laqgha ta' Djalogu mal-muzicisti.

(d) Ghajnuna lis-Socjetà ta' l-Arti, Manifattura u Kummerc billi l-Gvern baghat skrivan "*on secondment*" halli jghin fl-amministrazzjoni ta' din is-Socjetà.

(e) Ser jinfetah Muzew marittimu fil-Birgu u iehor dwar il-Medicina f'Santu Spirtu, Rabat.

(f) Zdied is-sussidju tal-kotba bil-Malti minn £M500 ghal £M800. Fi zmenijiet ohra dawn il-flus ma kienux jitqassmu.

(g) Ingab Malta *microfilm* ta' manuskritt tas-Seklu XVIII, dwar il-Lingwa Maltija misjub minn Dr. Arnold Cassola u aktar tard gie ppubblikat fi ktieb mill-Ministeru ta' l-Edukazzjoni.

(h) Sar kors itwal mis-soltu ghat-tahrig tal-vuci mill-Professoressa Bulgara Dobreva.

(i) Instab il-*Caravaggio* misruq.

Saturday, 4th

Director of Museum of Capodimonte, Professor Spinosa, visits Malta. Discuss the exhibition of works by Mattia Preti. Take him round to see paintings in churches.

Tuesday, 7th

I took Prof. Spinosa to see the 'St. Jerome'. He made some very interesting comments on previous restorations and offered to restore the painting in Naples.

Wednesday, 15th

After an exhibition at the Museum, I spoke very frankly to Dott. Romano of the Italian Embassy about the restoration of the Caravaggio. Why were things dragging on for long? Did one have to use tactics such as those used by Dom. Mintoff to get results?

Thursday, 16th

My outburst yesterday must have shaken my friend Dott. Romano.

He phoned today and told me that we could take the painting to Rome. He also told me that there was a military plane available but no civilian passenger would be allowed on board. I insist that we could not let the painting travel unaccompanied. A short time later he phoned saying that I could go but that I had to sign a document acknowledging that the Italian Government could not be held responsible for my personal safety.

I rushed off to tell the Minister. He replied, "One problem off my mind!"

I informed Mrs Dorigo and Prof Xausa [of the Italian Institute], both of whom had shown great interest in the painting.

Meanwhile, we prepared a box in which the 'St. Jerome' was to be packed for Rome.

We made contact with Rome to arrange for the arrival of the painting. We also asked the Ministry to insure the Caravaggio painting. The secretary informed me he would insure the painting for Lm1,000,000. I duly informed the Archbishop.

It was quite a shock when I got to know later that the painting had not been insured at all!!

The box containing the "St. Jerome" on a plane to Rome

Tuesday, 28th

Leave for Rome: five police vans with personnel carrying weapons accompanied the painting from the Depot in Floriana to the airport. My friend the forensic expert was there. Waited for two hours and finally boarded the twin engined military plane. The flight was quite rough and hot and there were no proper seats.

The box containing the Caravaggio painting was secured on top of some other luggage. I myself held tightly on to a strap for the duration of the flight.

We arrived quite late at Rome airport. There was Prof. Basile representing the Istituto Centrale del Restauro accompanied by armed police and a representative from our Embassy in Rome. It took some time to get through Customs. I got the impression that the Customs Officials had not been properly informed. The officer started reading rules about the importation of paintings. I told him that this was no ordinary painting – it was a Caravaggio!

Our intention was originally to follow the police to the Istituto to deliver the painting, but Prof. Basile assured us that there was no point as the staff at the Istituto had already left. I thought we would therefore see to matters in the morning but Prof. Basile insisted that it would not be possible as the morrow (the feast of SS. Peter and Paul) was a public holiday in Rome and there would still be no staff available at the Istituto.

I had to find a telephone booth as I had some urgent calls to make to Malta in connection with the delivery of the painting, so I asked to be dropped off at the Termini Station.

There were the usual long queues for the telephone booths. The first phone call that I made was to the Ministry. We had agreed that a person would stand by till I phoned and delivered the coded message - 'The book has arrived' and he would inform the Minister at once. I phoned the agreed telephone number numerous times but there was no reply. As a last resort I phoned my brother and asked him to get in touch with another secretary who could deliver the message. I then phoned Security at the Istituto, who assured me that the painting had been delivered and that I need not worry - 'Tutto a posto.' I had kept the key of the box containing the painting so that when the time came for the box to be unlocked, we would be present.

With my mind at rest that this important mission had been safely accomplished, I caught a train to Syracuse to get the ferry boat back to Malta. I was anxious to get back. I had to relay the information that all had gone well with the delivery of the painting to the *Istituto* and I was also due to enter hospital for an operation. I was travelling at my own expense and could not afford the time or luxuries usually allotted to government officials when travelling on work-related matters.

Wednesday, 29th

I arrived back in Malta safely and feeling perfectly happy – the Caravaggio is finally in Rome - and soon to be restored.

Or so I thought!

Tuesday, 12th

Attended the official opening of the Police Academy. Met Archbishop and gave him the most recent update on the 'St. Jerome' in Rome thinking that he had already been informed of the painting's recovery. When I referred to the final moments at the Police Depot, I told him that the Minister had insisted that he would inform the Archbishop himself of the good news. It seemed in fact that he had not. The Archbishop told me "Inti qed tghidli" (This is news to me).

Wednesday, 20th

Worked hard on the Exhibition Hall at the Auberge de Provence. Am looking forward to completing this project.

Friday, 22nd

I have already referred to the question of the Assistant Curator of Fine Arts. One post had been advertised in the Government Gazette – now two appointments had been given.

I sent the one I considered best to the Fine Arts Museum but I was still not happy with the way things were being done. The Minister continued to assure me that his "political acumen" would help solve the problem. I think he understood my worry. At one time he had phoned me personally to assure that the best candidate had come first in the written exam. At other times I almost got the blame for "being too honest". I'm still proud of that.

Meanwhile, I kept on working. Every time the Minister and his wife came to visit an exhibition I would show them the progress on the new Art Gallery. They were usually non committal, at least he was. On one occasion, the Minister showed unusual interest – he was looking up at the ceiling and at the walls. On closer enquiry it emerged that another M.P. had informed him of some dangerous

The opening of the Museum of Fine Arts

work being carried out by Fr. Zerafa that would inevitably bring down the Auberge!

This was the same M.P. who, on the day that the 'St. Jerome' was recovered, had tabled a question in the House suggesting that it was high time that the government paid the ransom money to get the painting back.

At this time the Minister came up with the idea of turning Villa Portelli into a Political Museum. The Political Museum in Vittoriosa had been a total disaster. I had other interests and anyway, nothing came of it. Besides, I was also beginning to take a very poor view of politics and politicians.

Tuesday, 2nd

A stab in the back – a most unkind act – ironically, almost a year to the date of the painting's recovery.

I was called to the Ministry of Foreign Affairs. There I met the Minister and his secretary, an old friend and schoolmate of mine. What he said startled me – at first I thought he was pulling my leg ... I thought it was just an introduction to something else that he wanted to tell me ... the Minister said that he had received a letter from the Maltese Embassy in Rome saying that I had abandoned the painting at the airport and just walked away! It took me some time to realise that he was serious.

I explained that I had handed over the painting to Prof. Basile, the official representative of the Istituto, and his armed escort as directed. Never for a moment did anyone suggest otherwise. Far from it!

I had then made sure that the painting had reached the Istituto and had phoned Malta to confirm this to the Ministry. I also mentioned that I had travelled at my own expense and no arrangements had been made for me to spend the night in Rome. This, I think, rather surprised him. In fact he made me promise that I would claim the expenses I had incurred - which of course I never did.

Even now, I cannot imagine what could have been behind this horrible calumny. I had risked my life for the painting, I had travelled to Italy on a military plane and then returned by train and ferry at my own expense yet here I was almost being accused of negligence!

The Minister, at least, appeared to understand the situation. I remember the words he used at the time.

The trouble-maker must have been some frustrated nobody wanting to bask in the success of the recovery – after all, what purpose was this accusation meant to serve? I felt it would have been better if our people in Rome had told their Minister what they had done (or not done) to hasten the painting's restoration all the while that it was just left shut away in a box.

My Minister would be present when the box was finally opened in our presence <u>many, many months</u> later. The '*St. Jerome*' was still wrapped in plastic! Nothing had been done to the painting at all! It does not take an expert to realise what it means to have an un-stretched canvas wrapped in plastic for any length of time in such a humid atmosphere as that of the Instituto in Rome.

Later on, I was able to tell our Ambassador in Rome what I thought of him while he was with my Minister in a Hotel in Florence. (He was presumably the same Ambassador who had written the letter saying that I had abandoned the painting.) The Minister was asking me to kindly procure some paintings for this Ambassador's office. Who had informed him, (or rather misinformed him) of what had happened at the airport?

On that occasion the Minister, who knew the facts, stood up for me. The Ambassador was very diplomatic. He said nothing.

'... *What a spider's web we weave, when first we practice to deceive...* '

Monday, 8th

A marble plaque was put up for my uncle Paul Boffa at the house in Vittoriosa, where he was born. I admired him most of all as a perfect gentleman and a dedicated doctor, so I resisted all attempts to turn it into a political event. The plaque went up – quietly and with no unnecessary fuss! Just 'Pawlu Boffa 1890 - 1962' the way he would have wanted it.

At this time the Headmaster of the Vittoriosa School had told my brother that there was talk of the school being named after my uncle. As I knew that this would require the approval of politicians, I was not over-optimistic.

Friday, 12th

Attempts to stop me and the work on the gallery continue. An unusually offensive and inaccurate letter from the Secretary of Din l-Art Helwa had been sent to the Ministry accusing the Curator of Archaeology of throwing away archaeological material. This was in fact just rubble that needed to be cleared to create the Exhibition Hall. I asked to meet the President of Din l-Art Helwa and, accompanied by a lawyer, insisted on a written apology. I got it.

Monday, 15th

I was present at Castille for a discussion on the Renzo Piano project for Valletta. The reaction was quite positive. I could however hear someone saying, sotto voce, "over my dead body."

Wednesday, 17th

Dinner at the Costa del Sol hosted by the Minister to thank the Police Commissioner and myself for our part in the recovery of the Caravaggio. I felt that I should tell my Minister that the Minister for Foreign Affairs had sent for me regarding the letter that had been received from our Embassy in Rome. My Minister was not amused. He told me that he should have been the first to be informed. During the dinner the Minister felt unwell, but I'm almost sure it was not the letter that caused it.

Friday – 26th

Again the 'scarlet letter'. At a reception at the British High Commission, I met my old friend the Foreign Minister's secretary. Naturally, I referred to the letter received from Rome. He told me to treat it with the contempt it deserved and offered to show me a copy of the letter he had sent by way of reply to them.

I think it is high time we turned to a lighter incident.

I was back at St. Luke's hospital. Before I left the Museum, I had arranged to have an old precious crucifix painted by *Polidoro da Caravaggio* and belonging to St. John's Co Cathedral, restored while in Naple for exhibition. I had agreed with my good friend Dominic Cutajar to pack it and deliver it to a boat that would take it to Naples.

At around midnight I had an urgent phone call from the Commissioner of Police. They got me out of bed and I was surprised to hear the Commissioner's excited voice telling me that, *"They have* tried to steal the Caravaggio again! But..." he added triumphantly, *"we have caught them and we have apprehended a man."* I asked him the man's name. It was Dominic Cutajar! Someone had spotted the huge box leaving St. John's and suspecting that the thieves, doing it in style this time, had phoned the police! My friend the Commissioner just could not understand why I was laughing. He had known a different person when the real Caravaggio was stolen!

Polidoro da Caravaggio crucifix at St. John's Co-Cathedral

Tuesday, 22nd

Noel Galea Bason Exhibition. Took the opportunity to insist in public that it was high time that the 'St. Jerome' was restored.

Monday, 28th

Mrs. Dorigo told me she had spoken to Prof. Basile about the 'St. Jerome'. She said that she had been told that restoration work was in progress and also that they would like me to go and see it - but not during the month of December.

Monday, 5th

My Minister phones me at my office from Castille half way through a Cabinet meeting. He tells me that 'they' want Spinola Palace.

Spinola Palace, an eighteenth century palazzo in the old fishing village of St. Julians, had been recently restored and set up with great team effort as a Museum of Contemporary Art. There were a number of disadvantages with the place – it was not central and it had a lot of steps but a lot of work had gone into it and the results were very satisfactory. All the same, I told the Minister we would let it go, on condition we got something better. Years before, I had set my eyes on the Barrakka Hall, an ex -Military Chapel near Castille.

Barrakka Hall had been used as a Sorting Office for some years. At a meeting of members of the Stamp Advisory Board, I had insisted with the Post Master General that the Hall be converted from a Sorting Office to an Art Exhibition Hall. It was spacious and a Museum on an open plan would have been ideal. There were two huge tunnels underneath the Hall which were full of rubbish but they could be cleared. I thought one tunnel that had a separate entrance could be used as a temporary exhibition hall, the other would be ideal as a restoration laboratory. It was very accessible and the Barrakka Gardens at the back, could be used for concerts and open air exhibitions. I was thinking of placing two busts at the entrance – one of Sciortino and one of Calì - to indicate its function as a gallery of contemporary Maltese Art.

The Minister, as usual, said yes.

The bust of Calì was eventually erected – at the back of the Barrakka Hall.

Wednesday, 28th

Quite by accident I met someone from the Rome Embassy at the Foundation for International Studies. I mentioned the letter from the Embassy and told him, "The truth will out!" He replied, "They knew what the Ambassador was like and yet they let him be!" He told me that he had asked about the Caravaggio and had been told it was being <u>fumigated</u>! Smoke screen indeed!

Back of Barrakka Hall showing Bust of Calì by V. Apap

Saturday, 28th

Today was the official inauguration of the exhibition hall at the Museum with an exhibition of paintings by Joseph Mallia. At the opening I mentioned the problems I'd been through until the Hall was completed. The Minister, as usual, was full of praise "...It was a job well done so I did not need to interfere".

I took advantage of the Minister's presence to explain my plans for the conversion of Barrakka Hall into a contemporary Art Museum. The Minister promised to help.

Everybody seemed to be satisfied with the new gallery and we soon had a long list of requests for exhibitions and lectures. As usual there was the odd man out. A particular "Disillusioned Art Critic" showed his disapproval in one of his articles in the press. I photocopied the article and stuck it up on the wall of the gallery for all to see-and-judge. Some time later while I was away, he visited the gallery and tore the article to shreds thus saving me the trouble to do so myself.

At the reception I discussed my designs on the conversion of Barakka hall into a Contemporary Art Museum and the Minister promised to help.

So much hard work had already gone into the preparation of the Art Museum at Spinola Palace! It would be a pity indeed if all that work was for nothing but it would be almost worth our while if we got a more suitable venue for the Modern Art Museum. Was a change of Government sufficient reason to close and not re-open a much needed Museum of Contemporary Art? Were we serious about wanting to promote art and help Maltese artists or not?

Tuesday, 14th

At a meeting of St. John's Cathedral Committee, I reminded the members of my repeated suggestion to move the paintings crowding the walls of the sacristy to the Carapecchia corridor. The corridor would form part of the Museum, provide a painting section and thus increase its attraction. I also produced a plan to show how visitors could enter the Oratory to visit the Caravaggio, and then see the tapestries upstairs before going downstairs to pass through the corridor into St. John's.

In return I was almost accused of being a fifth columnist making it easy to the government to lay hands on church property. Anyone who visits the Museum now will probably agree that it was not such a bad idea after all.

Friday, 24th

Met my Minister during a meeting at the Mnajdra Temples. We had submitted a project for its protection. He also told me that Barrakka Hall was 'in the bag.'

Thursday, 16th

Plans to dig a ditch around the Mnajdra Temples are still being discussed. Dr. Gouder (Curator of Archaeology*) and I write to the Minister to express our disapproval.*

Thursday, 30th

Leave for Paris with Konrad Buhagiar to order new tapestries for the Palace. Very lucky. Managed to find the firm that still had the patterns and sizes of the old tapestries ordered so many years before.

Prehistoric Altar in the Tarxien Room at the Museum of Archaeology

Sunday, 9th

Our first meeting with the new Director at the Italian Institute - a good man full of good intentions and bursting with ideas and projects. 'lingua insana in mente sana'. I made it very clear to him that if he wanted to help Malta he ought to start by hastening the restoration of our Caravaggio in Rome.

Tuesday, 18th

Mrs. Dorigo phones to tell me that something is being done about the 'St. Jerome'. She apologises for the delay by the Istituto di Restauro. I said I understood and spoke of 'Roma eterna'.

Wednesday, 19th

Minister called me to tell me that some silver had been stolen from St John's. After all the talk and bluff following the recovery of the 'St. Jerome', nothing – but nothing – had been done in the way of security! The thief had got in through one of the windows – the scaffolding had been conveniently left on the side of the Cathedral so that he could climb up to the window and then climb down one of the Baroque columns in the Chapel of the German Langue. I told the Police Commissioner that it had been so easy, thief would try it again.

(He did!!)

Met the Archbishop. He asked me about the 'St. Jerome'. I told him that nobody seemed to be interested. He was on a different wavelength; he was still worried that the painting would not return to St. John's – I was worried whether it was ever going to be restored or returned at all!

Tuesday, 25th

Another theft at St. John's. Resisted the temptation to say, 'I told you so!' Silver stolen. 'The Beheading' ... slashed! Words, words, words. Meeting with Minister and Commissioner of Police at Curia. I suggest a small task force responsible for security, closed circuit TV etc.

Police called me this evening. Two round paintings had been found at Manoel Island – probably a temporary hiding place before getting them off the island.

Wednesday, 26th

Invited to a discussion on National Treasures on TV – 'Nithadduha'. As usual spoke my mind. Said I'm sure that I'm just wasting my time. Nobody cares. Exploded when somebody asked about the restoration of the Caravaggio.

Saturday, 29th

Exhibition by an Italian artist.

I took advantage of the presence of the Italian Ambassador. He said, 'Tutti sentiamo la mancanza...della pittura'. (We all sorely feel the loss of the painting) The Minister butted in "Certamente non e' colpa del direttore." (It is certainly not the Director's fault).

I should hope so, too!

DES ON U.S. P, KILLS 47

WASHINGTON, April 19.' were killed aboard the U.S. n a big turret gun exploded the Atlantic, a Defence iid.

and Puerto Rican operating areas. The exercise began on April 13 and was to run through May 4.

It involves 29 U.S. ships along with Venezuelan and Brazilian frigates. Overall, 19,000 naval personnel are taking part in the exercise, military spokesmen said.

Defence Secretary Dick Cheney and Joint Chiefs of Staff Chairman Admiral William Crowe were informed of the incident while attending a NATO defence ministers' meeting in Brussels.

The *Iowa's* 16-inch guns are in three turrets. The explosion occurred in the number two turret. *(Reuter).*

TOURIST–DRUGGING GANG AT LARGE IN ISTANBUL

ISTANBUL, April 19.

A gang that has drugged, robbed and abandoned at least 20 foreign tourists this year is at large in Istanbul, consular sources said today.

Eleven victims of the gang were Japanese. Others included two British men, a British woman, a New Zealand woman, an American man and a Hungarian woman teacher who was also raped.

The gang is being blamed by some consulates for the death this month of 24-year-old Polish student Krzysztof Petykiewicz, Western consular officials said.

Polish Consul Jerzy Drozdz told Reuters Petykiewicz was drugged and robbed and that like other embassies, Poland was warning its nationals to take care. *(Reuter).*

Priceless ornaments stolen from Cathedral chapel

By a Staff Reporter

Priceless ornaments adorning the old icon of Our Lady of Carafa in the chapel of the Holy Sacrament at St. John's Co-Cathedral, in Valetta, were stolen on Tuesday evening.

The police are holding some persons to help them in their investigations.

The Co-Cathedral's sacristan discovered the effigy of Our Lady divested of its silver ornamental crest when he went to prepare for the 7.30 Mass yesterday morning.

Sources said that also missing was a gold cross which was removed from the door of the tabernacle and silver ornaments which were on the gate of the chapel.

A spokesman for the Cathedral said that the stolen items were of great historical value but the silver had little melt-down value.

The circumstances of how those

carrying out the theft entered the Cathedral were not immediately known yesterday.

Sources close to the police said that no signs of a break-in were found. Possibilities being considered include that of someone remaining inside the Cathedral when it was closed on Tuesday evening.

Another possibility is that the thief could have made use of the scaffolding on the facade of the Co-Cathedral which is being restored.

Magistrate Dr. Patrick Vella yesterday held an inquiry at the Co-Cathedral. On the site soon after the theft was discovered were Archbishop Mgr. Mercieca, the Vicar General Mgr. Annetto Depasquale, and Police Commissioner Mr. Alfred Calleja who is heading Police investigations on the theft. Forensic experts from the Police laboratory are helping in the investigations.

During the time of the Knights the chapel of the Blessed Sacrament, formerly known as

(Cont. back page col. 2)

MAN MISSING SINCE FRIDAY

By a Staff Reporter

The police yesterday traced the car belonging to Marcellino Dowling, 31, of Gharghur, who has been missing from home since last Friday. The car, a white Toyota, was found at Selmun in the morning. Its doors were locked.

Dowling, who was still unaccounted for by late yesterday evening, went out at about 3 p.m. on Friday after telling his mother that he was going to buy something.

The man is 160cm tall and has brown eyes. He was reported wearing a stone washed jeans, a green jacket, a beige vest and training shoes. The Police are investigating.

A picture of part of the chapel of the Blessed Sacrament (from Dominic Cutajar's book on "History and works of art of St. John's Church, Valetta") showing the icon of Our Lady of Carafa, the tabernacle and the chapel gate, which were the target of thieves on Tuesday night. On right, the Archbishop, Mgr. Mercieca, leaving St. John's Co-Cathedral after inspecting the burgled chapel.

The Times - Thursday, April 20, 1989

The exhibition was followed by luncheon at the Casino Maltese. I sat next to the Italian Ambassador. We continued our discussion. I told him that Mintoff did not have to wait this long to have _two_ Caravaggio paintings restored. Mr. Suzanni stood by and supported me. He had spoken to friends of Sen. Andreotti to get things moving. The Italian Ambassador tried to be helpful. He said that he was willing to pay for the restoration out of his own pocket. He did point out, however, that it was up to us to do something about it. "After all" he said "it is _your_ painting".

40   THE TIMES, FRIDAY, JULY 5, 1991

Suspended jail sentence for "national heritage jewel" thief

A former health assistant, found guilty of trying to steal Caravaggio's "Beheading of St. John" and of stealing priceless items, considered to be part of the national heritage, from St. John's co-Cathedral, Valletta in 1989, was yesterday jailed for two years, the judgment being suspended for four years.

Caravaggio's painting had suffered irreparable damage when accused, Ivan Grima, 23 of Marsascala, had slashed it with a surgical knife stolen from St. Luke's Hospital where he was employed in the casualty department.

Magistrate Dr. Patrick Vella said in the judgment that on the night of April 18 1989, Grima stole a silver armour covering the painting of Our Lady of Carafa; two silver ornaments forming part of the gate leading to the Chapel of the Sacrament; and a silver cross.

Five days later, on the night of April 24, the accused also stole an icon representing Our Lady. He even tried to steal the painting representing the beheading of St. John, causing it irreparable damage in the process.

Magistrate Vella said that although the items stolen were valued altogether at about Lm6,100, in fact they are considered by arts experts as priceless items from all aspects as they form part of the country's national heritage.

All items were found by the police at Grima's residence on May 27, 1989. A piece of wood, forming part of the painting of Our Lady of Carafa, was also found in a garage used by the accused at Birkirkara.

SIGNED PAINTING

The damage to Caravaggio's painting was done by a surgical knife, which was found by the police near the same painting. Someone had tried to cut out the painting from its frame in order to roll it up and steal it.

As correctly stated by the court-appointed expert, Antonio Espinosa Rodriguez, the 1608 painting is the only work of art signed by Caravaggio and is also considered among his best masterpieces.

Its artistic value placed it first among Malta's works of art and among the best masterpieces throughout the world. Thus, no commercial value could be established.

The court pointed out that the cut caused by the surgical knife was actually made on Caravaggio's signature, thus causing permanent damage to the painting.

Magistrate Vella said it was proved by the court-appointed fingerprint experts that fingerprints of the accused matched those found on parts of gloves found on the scene of the crime.

SERIOUS PROBLEM

Defence counsel had submitted that the fingerprints experts' evidence should be disregarded on the basis of other court judgments, including the Constitutional Court, where proof produced by experts who formed part of the police force or fell under the responsibility of the Commissioner of Police was ruled out.

"The court would like to point out," Magistrate Vella said, "That the issue over fingerprint experts has become a serious problem to the administration of justice. The problem needs to be urgently settled and in the most practical way."

He added that the problem had placed in a very unhappy situation all the judges in the country. On the other hand, one had to be reasonable, in the sense that no other fingerprints experts are available except those in the police force.

The court, however, felt that in

Magistrate Vella also referred to statements made by Grima after his arrest. Grima had admitted to all the thefts except to the damage caused to Caravaggio's painting. Accused insisted he had only provided the surgical knife and gloves, which were easily available to him since he worked as a health assistant at St. Luke's Hospital's casualty department.

The court added it did not even have the most remote moral or rational doubt that it was Grima who committed the crime. It was also convinced that more than one person was involved, the accused being one of them.

On inflicting punishment, the court considered that the thefts took place within one week and caused great uproar on the Island. Furthermore, the thefts took place at St. John's Co-Cathedral "a most precious jewel in the historic and national heritage".

Those who committed the theft demonstrated great courage and at the same time challenged twice the Maltese society, which, in this case, was the real victim of the crime.

But the court also considered the absolute good conduct of the accused and his young age. The court felt it proper to give Grima a chance to reform himself.

Dr. Albert Libreri was defence counsel.

Police Inspectors Raymond Vella Gregory and Joseph Valletta prosecuted.

Call for inquiry on cost over-runs at Zammit Clapp Hospital

and the present minister could not

PSST! Will we be suspended too? (With apologies to Cavaggio's Beheading)

Caravaggio at slashed prices!

Tuesday, 9th

Discuss project of Central Bank.

Friday, 12th

Went to visit my Minister with the Curator of Archaeology. Am pleased to hear that there is finally an agreement about <u>not</u> having a ditch dug around Mnajdra Temples. I ask what is being done about the security at St. John's Co Cathedral.

In fact nothing was being done so, at a St. John's Committee meeting, I suggest that we make a formal protest about the lack of security as well as the restoration delay.

Saturday, 13th

At a reception at the German Ambassador's residence today, I told my Minister that the Director of the Capodimonte Museum has offered to have the 'St. Jerome' restored at his museum and that the Italian Ambassador has offered to pay for it. I advise against this but point out that something must be done! He suggests we discuss the matter with the Chapter of St. John.

Tuesday, 16th

Dott.Romano from the Istituto phones to tell me that work has finally started on the painting. There had been problems of money. After all those excuses... It was a question of money! Why did it have to take all this time to get the finances approved?

This had not happened when the two Caravaggio paintings had

been restored in Rome in the fifties. It was not to happen when the
'*Beheading*' was restored in Florence. What was our Ministry, what
were our men in Rome doing all this time?! Had the fumigation been
a smoke screen?!

Later, I said this much and more to the Minister when I
referred to the report from the Istituto.

Wednesday, 17th

My Minister asks me to allow a member of staff access again to a
telephone in the Museum. This member of staff had used the phone
far too often to conduct his private business and a previous Minister
had asked me to remove this privilege.

Thursday, 25th

Flight to Rome.

Friday, 26th

I visited the Istituto del Restauro in Rome to see the 'St. Jerome'.
I met a friend I had known for years there. She was very apologetic
but was told that I simply could not see the painting. The excuse
was that they were very busy with classes!

Whilst in Rome I had been to lunch at Dott. Vattani`s house in
Trastevere. There I met Dott Spinosa. We spoke about the Preti
exhibition and spoke at length with Dott. Vattani regarding the
restoration of the '*St. Jerome*'.

Saturday, 27th

*Received a phone call from Police Depot at 5.30 pm. The silver
that had been stolen from St. John's Co Cathedral has been
returned. Yet another story that still needs to be told.*

Tuesday, 30th

*The Italian Ambassador phoned to tell me that the restoration of
the 'St. Jerome' will be completed within the year.*

many years you can testify that this is not something I am
raking up now but something I have been insisting on for
years. I think you should be provided with all the facts;
I think it is time they were put on record and made known
to all concerned.

I feel it is a national disgrace that the "St Jerome" should
be hidden away in a box where it can suffer damage while
Maltese and foreign art lovers are deprived of this unique work
of art. How anyone could be so callously cynical about these
things, especially after all the flagwaving and solemn speeches
we had after its return to Malta, is just beyond me. I'm finding
it very difficult to explain to people who write from abroad to
enquire about its whereabouts; I was particularly embarrassed
recently when the matter came up in the presence of a foreign
ambassador whom I had pestered for months on end and who had in
fact done a lot to have the painting restored.

I thought that after the long agony we had been through the matter
would soon be brought to a satisfactory conclusion. You know the
hard time we had - I will pass over my part in the matter- but
I can assure you that it was a difficult and thankless task. In
this latter connection, I think two very unpleasant facts should
be put on record. These, I am sure, should not be forgotten or
condoned.

The first concerns our diplomatic representative in Rome. You
know I had volunteered to take the painting in a military plane
to Rome at a time when I was not feeling well at all and was
supposed to be in hospital. When I arrived at Rome airport I

Letter to the Ministry

Monday, 5th

Dott. Vattani phoned from Rome to tell me that the 'St. Jerome' restoration is definitely in progress.

Friday, 9th

I had a meeting with my Minister and two Monsignori to discuss security at St. John's. We mention tapestries, marble tombstones, night watchman and the placing of iron bars in windows. Then Reverend members drifted off to complain about more trivial matters.

Around this time I wrote a strong letter to the Ministry about the delay in restoring the painting. I described it as 'A National Disgrace'.

It was not unknown at this time to be told that letters intended for the Ministry would not arrive. Quite often I would keep a copy of these letters in my pocket and hand them personally to the Minister when he came to the Museum.

Monday, 19th

At an opening of an exhibition I spoke about the restoration of the St. Jerome in public in the presence of my Minister and the Italian Ambassador. Everyone burst out clapping – a feeling of some support!

Wednesday, 28th

Spoke to Minister re Hypogeum and Barrakka Hall.

Friday, 7th

My Minister asks me to go to Taverna, Italy with him.

Monday, 17th

Meeting at St. John's. I insisted we should revive Church State Committee on St. John's. Would save a lot of problems later on.

Met experts from New York re 'The Beheading'. Took them out to lunch. Agreed unanimously that painting would not benefit from being sent abroad.

Tuesday, 18th

Went to speak to Minister re Barrakka Hall. Also told him that the Antiquities Board is not functioning at all. I received quite a volte face – do you think I should quarrel with other ministers just to please you?! No Minister. Definitely not.

Wednesday, 19th

Today we finally held a meeting on security at St. John's. It was attended by my Minister, the Minister for Justice, the Commissioner of Police, and a couple of Monsignors. I suggested iron bars on windows, punch clocks for watchmen, tinted glass in chapels, and protection of marble tomb stones. The Police have promised to install a direct phone line to the Depot and to have police officers patrol the area regularly.

I still thought it should go to the Oratory. Documents connected with Caravaggio could be displayed there and the

Oratory could be the 'Sancta Sanctorum' of Caravaggio.

The Oratory had been the centre of Caravaggio's life for a year. There he had been received as a knight; there he had produced his masterpiece and there too, he had been expelled from the Order.

At one time we had organised a big Caravaggio exhibition in the Oratory with original Manuscripts and photographs of works. It had been a huge success. We had also included a portrait of Caravaggio last discovered at the Archibishop's Palace at Mdina.

Thursday, 27th

Phone call from the Ministry of Justice asking me to appear on T.V. to say that the Monti (Valletta Market Stalls) should no longer be set up opposite St. John's Co Cathedral.

Exhibition on Caravaggio manuscripts and photos - The Oratory of St. John

Friday, 4th

Leave at 9.30 with Minister for Rome.

Rather than go straight through airport as an ordinary mortal, had to endure much protocol – because I was with the Minister.

In Rome we stayed at the luxury Bernini Hotel but said Mass at the poor Capuchin Church. The Minister read the lessons.

Minister hires a car and drives us all the way to Taverna where we arrive rather late.

Saturday, 5th

We sign a gemellaggio (twinning) between the town of Taverna, Preti's birthplace and Zurrieq where the artist is said to have spent some time. I give a conference on Preti at St. Dominic's church to a full audience who become a full congregation when I later say Mass for them. Many favourable comments but the Minister's wife is not sure about the cut of my shirt.

Monday, 7th

Drive off from Taverna. Stop in Naples to see the Pretis before returning to Rome.

Tuesday, 8th

Go to the Istituto Centrale to see the 'St. Jerome'. We were met by a junior restorer who rambled on about some elementary restoration procedures to the Minister. Finally, he asked an assistant to bring the box containing the painting. Immensely shocked when the box was opened and we saw our painting still un-stretched, un-restored and still in the plastic cover in which it had been wrapped in Malta. What an anti climax!

To show my anger and disapproval, I turned away and took some photos from a distance as I thought this event ought to be recorded.

Saw the "Aida" at Caracalla. Hardly in the mood for a triumphant march.

Returned to Malta a sadder and a wiser man.

Wednesday, 16th

The Minister tells me that he has received news re progress on the restoration of 'St. Jerome'. He also tells me that he was promised the painting would be ready in November! I could hardly believe what I heard after what I had seen.

Thursday, 17th

The Commissioner of Police tells me he has information that there are plans to rob the church of St. James in Valletta. I inform the Vicar General and remove a painting of St. James by Paladini from the Church.

Later on I would lend this painting to the Apostolic Delegate to block up an unsightly window at his residence during the Pope's visit there. I was told later that the Pope admired it.

Friday, 18th

A silly project is being proposed to move all monuments of past Prime Ministers of Malta to Castille Square. I am totally against it.

Tuesday, 22nd

Meeting on security at the Ministry. The Minister had somehow commissioned an English expert to conduct a study on security for St. John's. He promised to let me have a look at it - but in fact never did. When I caught a glimpse of it, it looked very elaborate with drawings and diagrams, but when I asked about security in the Chapel of 'St. Jerome', I was told that 'St. Jerome' had not even been taken into consideration! In fact it was never mentioned again the report. This report like so many others was just a waste of time and money and like so many others died a natural death.

I still insisted on having a watchman sleep in the room in St. John's designed by the Knights, precisely for this purpose.

This room overlooks the interior of St. John's and was made use of in the past - there was no reason why we could not do so now. A direct line to the Depot could provide additional security. The watchman inside need not have to confront an intruder. Quite safe from inside this room, he would be able to press a buzzer connected to the Police Depot.

Wednesday, 23rd

The Prime Minister's assistant asked me to take part in a discussion on TV on the Piano Project for Valletta with Architect Buhagiar,

Dr.Caruana Curran and Architect Valentino. He also asked me to organise an exhibition of the Piano Project, complete with models and plans in the new gallery.

Friday, 25th

Meeting of Heads at the Ministry. I insist on sufficient wardens for all cultural sites.

The Prime Minister came to the Museum to see the Piano Project exhibition; he spoke to journalists and sounded very positive about the project.

Thursday, 31st

Attend presentation of certificates to guides by my Minister. I mentioned once more that we should do something about the Hypogeum.

The Hypogeum would have to wait for years. The fact that the Hypogeum is what it is today is only due to the determination and patience of Dr. Gouder, Curator of Archaeology, along with the full support of his Minister at the time.

Artist impression of Piano's City Gate

Friday, 1st

Meeting at St. John's.

Remind them once more about reviving Government/Church Committee to avoid problems in future.

Spoke of security and protection of marble tombstones. Describe the method used in Siena Cathedral.

The protection of the tombstones in St. John's is an old problem. In the past, a number of "marmisti" had been employed to carry out ongoiong restoration. These had later been taken by Government to carry out other unconnected with St. John's. Concerts and other activities were held frequently at St. John's and the tombstones suffered accordingly.

Every now and then some bright idea for the solution of the problem would appear in the press. A fancy project with plastic sheeting, complete with drawings and diagrams did the rounds. Then, suddenly expensive carpets appeared, these were removed equally suddenly as they were doing more harm than good. In brief, it was one long story of hard headedness and amateurism, alternating with a couldn't-care-less attitude.

Saturday, 9th

Du Cros exhibition in the New Gallery at the Auberge de Provence.

Some years ago I had seen a huge collection of oil and water-colour paintings at the Lausanne Museum in Switzerland. I thought it would be wonderful to exhibit them in Malta and arranged to meet Madame Pometta, the Swiss Ambassador in Rome. She kindly accepted to send the collection over, which included some very interesting drawings of Valletta.

Saturday, 16th

Big exhibition - Malta Through the Ages – in the Salon of the Auberge de Provence.

Thursday, 21st

25th Anniversary of Malta's Independence. Celebrations. Take Senator Spadolini round St. John's. Has some very interesting comments to make. Had lunch with him at Italian embassy. Later unveiled a plaque at the 'Borsa' [Malta Chamber of Commerce and Industry] in Republic Street, Valletta.

Wednesday, 27th

A convoy memorial is being proposed. Have been asked to become a member of the committee. To discuss with the Sculptor, Sandle, the bonze figure forming part of the memorial.

Friday, 29th

Another meeting of Heads of Department. I again spoke about the Hypogeum and the Barrakka Hall. These Heads of Department all meeting in the Minister's office may have looked quite impressive, like an army set in array – but in fact I think it was just a waste of time. Those present had very different interests and needs. One hardly had the time to put in a request for one's particular department and there was a tendency to be interrupted by people who knew little and probably cared less about the point one was trying to make. I just could not afford to waste hours learning about kindergartens, benches etc. so I arranged with my secretary to phone me after half an hour and tell me that something terrible had happened at the Museum so I could get away.

Thursday, 26ᵗʰ

*Inauguration of a Boffa Exhibition at the Municipal Palace,
Merchants Street. I exhibited objects and mementos associated
with my uncle - letters, paintings, decorations etc. Probably the
prize exhibit was a collection of letters of appreciation sent to the
press about him after his death. The exhibition was opened by the
Minister of Foreign Affairs, Prof. De Marco. He spoke of Boffa as
the man who brought the idea of social justice into Malta and
described him as 'a great Christian democrat'.*

Opening of Boffa Exhibition

I had always looked upon Prof. De Marco as a true friend who
had always been good to me.

My Minister used to tease me, joking that my first loyalties
were with Prof. De Marco and not with him.

Monday, 6th

Isabel Borg exhibition.

Show my Minister a bozzetto for the Tarxien War Memorial. He tells me not to approve it.

Later, I would receive a copy of an angry letter received at Castille, complaining that ministers had admired the bozzetto but Fr. Zerafa had been difficult and had stopped the project! Naturally, I wrote back and explained.

Asked Minister to approve my project for a new base for the Boffa Monument. He signed willingly.

The monument had been set up 15 years before under Mintoff's Government and had been inaugurated by Dr. Buttigieg, (Chairman of a Committee that I belonged to).

The public had been very generous and could afford a proper monument. With the money left over, I commissioned my friend, the artist Pitré, to paint a portrait to be placed in Castille. There is a special account in the bank with the money that was left over.

The first idea was to have the monument near Portes Des Bombes and the Minister for Works had already had the platform site marked. I had insisted it should be put up near Victory Church. My friend, Dr. Buttigieg had promised to consult Mintoff. He had said it would be a good idea but, 'mur biddillu l-ideja lil dak ix-xadin!' (it would not be so easy to change his mind).

Later Dr. Buttigieg phoned to say, "You are lucky; Mintoff said 'go ahead". As he saw us working on the platform, Mintoff would call me up to his office and offer suggestions or instructions. His aesthetic views were not impressive, not even acceptable, but otherwise he did not obstruct at all. The main problem was that he believed monuments should be placed at ground level. He had his way in the case of Dimech. In the case of Boffa we haggled a lot. I insisted on 7ft but as usual he played around. He would have a 3ft base on top of a platform that was 4ft high!

As regards the inscription on the base he had insisted that I should include Boffa's knighthood. Naturally, he had his own reasons for wanting this. He had wanted me to put down that he was Prime Minister etc. I insisted that the more lapidary the inscription the more effective it would be. I mentioned Churchill and others who did not even have their Christian name inscribed. He saw he was getting nowhere and addressed me solemnly "Dun!" he said "In twenty years' time people will forget what your uncle has done, what I have done, what you have done!" Anyhow, finally it was "Pawlu Boffa 1890-1962".

I was still not satisfied with the height of the base. Years later, the Torpedo Depot was being dismantled and blocks of hard stone were going to be thrown away. I asked the architect in charge to preserve them on Manoel Island and 15 years later, I designed a new, higher base-worthy of the work of Vincent Apap, worthy of Paul Boffa. This did not happen without the usual problems. Someone from the Ministry told me that Boffa should not go higher than Borg Olivier. The architect assisting me was given similar instructions.

Later on, someone taking the Prime Minister's name in vain, came to office to tell me that the Prime Minister did not see the need for such a high base. That really threw me into a rage. I declared that I was resigning that very moment. The person who brought the message was so taken aback that he made a silent exit.

Inauguration of Boffa Monument

Things, as usual, eventually worked out satisfactorily. The Prime Minister came to the Museum for the launching of a book on Mattia Preti. They were projecting a video on Preti, the hall was crowded. I edged my way to where the Prime Minister was standing and tackled him about the Boffa Monument. He was extremely good about it. He said that nobody had mentioned anything to him and he had not expressed any idea at all. He said that he had no objection to what I was planning to do. In fact he suggested that I should install suitable lighting...

Wednesday, 15th

Meeting at the Ministry to discuss 'estimates'. I insist we should do something about the Hypogeum, security at St. John's and again about the Barrakka Hall. I felt the Maritime Museum in Vittoriosa, was what was uppermost on the Minister's mind.

Friday, 17th

Meeting at the Finance Department. I again insist on the Hypogeum Project and on security as top priorities.

Monday, 27th

Bush – Gorbachev Summit Meeting. Lunchtime Concerts at the Archaeology Museum.

Saturday, 2nd

Never had such bad weather as we do now during Bush – Gorbachev Summit Meeting!

Am asked to be at St. John's as Mrs. Gorbachev would like to visit the Cathedral.

The day before this, I had received a phone call from our Ambassador who asked me to suggest a place of interest for her to visit. He warned me, however, that she was not keen on visiting churches (which was strange, considering she had been to St. Peter's the day before). Also, she did not want to have priests around her. In fact if I were to take her round I was not to wear my clerical collar. I told him, nicely but firmly, that I hated nothing more than my plastic clerical collar and would not like to see it on my own dog, but I would not let anyone tell me what to do. I said quite simply that if she was not interested in St. John's Co Cathedral, well, I was not interested in her. I calmed down and next morning, there I was

With Mrs. Gorbachev at St. John's

waiting, with a whole line of Monsignori and dignitaries, for the arrival of Mrs. Gorbachov.

Mrs. Gorbachov failed to turn up, so I thought I would just come back to the Priory and have a rest.

At 3 p.m. I had an urgent phone call from the Prime Minister's office asking me to rush to St. John's Co Cathedral because Mrs. Gorbachov was already there. I said I had no car. "No problem, we will send you a car."

I got to St. John's. The Prime Minister's wife and daughter were already there and Mrs. Gorbachov had just arrived. The main door of the Cathedral was locked and the sacristan was nowhere in sight. We eventually managed to get in through a side door.

Before I left the Priory, I had had what turned out to be a good idea. I had already put a gold - plated, silver filigree Malta Cross in my pocket (this is always a welcome memento of Malta and I'm always well stocked with them) but then, I thought of something better. I did not want her to think I was some sort of medieval monk with book, bell and candle - a latter day Rasputin. Some years ago, way back in 1974 I had been a co-founder of the Maltese-Soviet Friendship Society, quite a mad thing to do in those days but

Russian Diploma

something I'm still proud of. Then, few years ago, I had received a Diploma – quite impressive, with Lenin's portrait on top and signed by the first female astronaut, Valentina Tereschova. I folded this into my pocket just before the driver arrived to take me to St. John's. The Monsignori that had lined up in the morning were not there "Flavit Deus et dissipati sunt" . So I had Mrs. Gorbachev more or less to myself. I apologised for the weather but said that we reserved this kind of weather for very special guests. The last time we used it was when St. Paul came to Malta. I showed her the Diploma and she immediately recognised the signature. "That's a famous signature." she said. I said "I want another famous signature!" and she signed it. I gave her the cross; she gave me a book on Russian Sacred Art. We went round St. John, which she found very interesting and she asked all the right questions. She read the inscriptions on the tombstones and impressed me by quoting Petrarch. Finally, she said "I will never forget this place". That is more or less the opening I had been waiting for. I said "If you ever forget it and would like to revive memories, just go to the Hermitage. There is a painting by Favray that depicts the interior of St. John's Co Cathedral in detail. To tell you the truth, the Maltese would love to borrow it." She said "Why don't you ask for it?"

We did - when we were planning the opening of the new Russian Centre in Merchant Street. The painting arrived, beautifully restored, in a special plane, and we exhibited it in the Centre and later in the Fine Arts Museum.

In his autobiography, Mr. Gorbachov says that he saw miles of rubble walls in Malta, while his wife was taken to see the island's treasures.

Thursday, 7th

Am consulted by President as to what gift to present to the Pope. I suggest a crucifix by the Maltese sculptor Josef Kalleja. Promise to prepare a special box for it.

Saturday, 16

Am still all for the Central Bank Project but someone in authority says 'over my dead body'. Reminds me of earlier reactions to Piano Project.

Wednesday, 27th

Meet my good friend Monsignor Calleja. We are to organise competitions producing memorabilia in connection with the Pope's forthcoming visit.

We are to select a portrait, a medal and a logo.

Wednesday, 3rd

Went to Rome and then on to Taverna to launch a new book on Mattia Preti. I was accompanied by Dr. and Mrs. R. Farrugia.

Thursday, 4th

On the way back from Taverna to Rome, got on plane with pipe, stick, and books but someone had left his case in the aisle. I tripped over it and hit my forehead on the hand-rest of seat. Lots of blood. Mrs. Farrugia was terrified. Plane informed Rome airport and an ambulance was standing by on arrival. Taken to emergency and had 6 or 7 stitches. Refused anaesthetic. Doctor asked me if it hurt. I said 'No'. He said "Lei è un bugiardo." Told me it will leave a mark. It seems my head can take anything!

Friday, 19th

Received letter from Istituto Del Restauro in Rome. The 'St. Jerome' will be back in March.

Friday, 26th

Meeting of Heads of Department. I firmly insist with Minister on having an iron fence constructed around Mnajdra. The Minister said, "I'll have to wait till there is someone available." Not quite sure what he means. Naturally, nothing was done.

Later on, some vandals removed some stones prompting a massive public reaction. Everyday letters appeared in the press and protestors marched down Republic Street with the authorities at their head. The ex-curator and myself refused to take part in the show. Instead, I wrote a letter to the press saying we had been talking too much and doing too little.

Thursday, 8th

It seems that someone in Rome was planning to send the restored 'St. Jerome' to Genoa before coming to Malta. I opposed this strongly.

Tuesday, 20th

Presented another memorandum to my Minister on what I believe are the immediate needs of the museums.

Popular appeal for justice - from Fr. Zerafa

Wednesday, 7th

Again a phone call from Rome saying that the 'St. Jerome' is going to Genoa. I am still very strongly against it.

Finally the painting was restored, exhibited at the Barberini Gallery and then brought back to Malta. I went to Rome with the Commissioner of Police and his wife. We returned, together with the Italian Minister, Dott. Facchiani, in a special plane. As we drank champagne and made merry at Rome Airport, it suddenly occurred to me that the box containing the 'St. Jerome' was too big to go into the plane. The painting had been put into a box that was then placed into a larger box. Rubber balls filling the spaces between the two boxes acted as shock absorbers for the painting. It was one of those things which had seemed like a good idea at the time but was now obviously unsuitable because of the size of the larger box.

We had no alternative but to remove the painting from the outer box and hold it next to us as we flew back to Malta.

It seemed that misfortune had to dog the 'St. Jerome' to the very end.

Monday, 23rd

The painting of the 'St. Jerome' is returned to Malta and is exhibited at the Police Headquarters until someone decides on its final resting place.

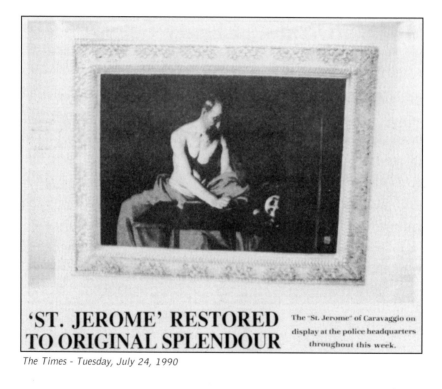

'ST. JEROME' RESTORED TO ORIGINAL SPLENDOUR

The "St. Jerome" of Caravaggio on display at the police headquarters throughout this week.

The Times - Tuesday, July 24, 1990

Saturday, 6th

Finally! The 'St. Jerome' was hung in the Chapel of Italy in St. John's! I was not invited for the occasion but friends informed me and I was there – hidden from sight, but feeling immensely proud.

In-Nazzjon Taghna - Saturday, April 6, 1991

Later on experts from Florence would point out that the strong rays of the sun through the window were causing damage to the painting. I had always been against hanging it so high up in the chapel. I had also been concerned about the risk to the painting from the strong light that would fall on it. Nobody listened. Somebody in authority actually justified the painting's presence there. He

RAFSANJANI ATTACKS OPPONENTS

NICOSIA.

Iran's pragmatist President Ali Akbar Hashemi Rafsanjani yesterday launched a scathing attack on his hardline rivals.

Rafsanjani called for closer relations with the outside world, saying Iran could not survive without

Fr. Marius Zerafa, the Director of Museums points out a detail in the restored painting of St. Jerome by Michelangelo Merisi de Caravaggio. The painting was officially handed back to Malta yesterday. At a brief ceremony at the Police Headquarters, Dott. Ferdinando Facchiano, the Italian Minister of Culture, returned the painting to Dr. Ugo Mifsud Bonnici, the Minister of Education and the Interior. The "St. Jerome" was stolen from St. John's Co-Cathedral in 1984 and recovered by the police in 1987. It was badly damaged and sent to Italian "Istituto Centrale del Restauro" for professional restoration.

(See story on page 17)

The Times - Tuesday, July 24, 1990

proclaimed (I do not know on whose authority) that Caravaggio had actually painted the '*St. Jerome*' to be placed precisely there. I would later referred to this as political license, covering a multitude of sins. The '*St. Jerome*' would later be removed to St. John's Oratory while the '*Beheading of St. John the Baptist*' was being restored in Florence. It was felt that finances would suffer if tourists were not made to pay to see it in the Oratory.

When '*The Beheading of St. John*' was returned from

Florence, there were attempts to take the '*St. Jerome*' back to the Chapel of Italy. Letters in favour of this were written to the newspapers, but finally good sense prevailed and the '*St. Jerome*' stayed in the Oratory of St. John's.

When The '*St. Jerome*' was restored at the Istituto Centrale in Rome, the authorities had insisted (in writing) that once it was back home, the painting was in no condition to travel again. It is sincerely hoped that this sagacious advice will be seriously adhered to.

There the '*St. Jerome*' now stands, awaiting a final judgement as regards a proper setting that will satisfy security, as well as aesthetic standards.

Let its memory rest,
Till other times are come,
And other men,
Who then may do it justice.

Thank God!

Chapter 8

BROUGHT BACK ON A GOLDEN PLATTER

Tuesday, 15th

The happy day has finally dawned.

I had taken the '*Beheading*' to Florence on an Italian vessel, the "Cassiopeia", to Livorno and then to Florence. It was exhibited in the Sala del Cinquecento in the Palazzo Vecchio and we managed to get the 'Sleeping Cupid' from the Uffizi and the 'A Knight of Malta' from the Pitti exhibited on either side of the '*Beheading*'. An official booklet published for the occasion, stated that the '*The Beheading of St. John*' would most probably be restored in Rome. I was not

Caravaggio's masterpiece on way to Italy

The Times - Monday, June 10, 1996

Caravaggio *Beheading* gives Malta flavour to EU summit

Veltroni promises greater support for Malta

Laurence Grech
in Florence

Malta was the toast of Florence yesterday, as the prime minister, Dr Eddie Fenech Adami, inaugurated a special show at the art capital's Palazzo Vecchio devoted to one of the island's major art treasures – Caravaggio's *The Beheading of St John*.

The painting, beautifully illuminated and temporarily restored, is the centre of attraction in the magnificent *Salone dei Cinquecento* and to accommodate it, a sculpture by Michelangelo, representing Victory – one of the many works of art by him and other masters filling the spacious hall – had to be hidden from view, at least for the three months the Malta exhibition will be on show.

Before the inauguration proper, the Caravaggio was admired by Italian Prime Minister Romano Prodi, who paid a fleeting visit to Palazzo Vecchio, seat of the Florence city council, at about 3 p.m. Florence today hosts the European Union summit, a gathering of the 15 heads of government of EU member states, and also the heads of government of 11 other states, including Central and Eastern European states, which all aspire to EU membership, besides Cyprus and Malta.

(Continued on page 20)

Walter Veltroni, the Italian deputy prime minister, said Italy was committed to press for Malta's membership of the European Union and promised to continue with its efforts to smooth the process of Malta's integration in Europe.

Mr Veltroni was speaking at the inauguration of the Malta Caravaggio exhibition at the Palazzo Vecchio in Florence yesterday, which he hailed as a symbol of the close relationship which the two countries enjoy.

Earlier Mr Veltroni said he was extremely pleased at this show of collaboration between Malta and Italy, and it was especially significant that this great painting came from Malta to Florence for the EU summit, thus underlining Malta's European aspirations and Italy's support for the island's efforts to give them full expression.

(Continued on page 17)

It was Malta day in Florence yesterday, as the art city welcomed Caravaggio's *The Beheading of St John* at a special show at Palazzo Vecchio. Prime Minister Eddie Fenech Adami is here seen at the opening of the exhibition.

The Times - Friday, June 21, 1996

keen on the idea – I was afraid that the painting was in no state to travel all the way to Rome and besides, the sad experience of the 'St. Jerome' was still all too vivid in my memory. The restorers at the *Pietre Dure* in Florence were very keen to carry out the restoration but they said that they would need permission from their Minister for Culture. As luck would have it, Signor Veltroni, the Minister for Culture, was present at the exhibition. While we were enjoying a pleasant conversation in front of *'the Beheading'*, he asked me where the restoration was going to take place. *"Perche' non a Firenze?"* I asked. Five minutes later, Signor Veltroni was up on the rostrum with our Prime Minister and our Minister for Foreign Affairs, saying how happy and honoured they would be to have the painting restored in Florence.

The painting did in fact undergo a Florentine restoration – the best it has ever had. When the restoration was complete, the 'Beheading of St. John' was exhibited for one month in the Carmine in a chapel opposite another chapel with the Masaccio frescoes.

I went up to Florence again and returned with the painting on another Italian cruiser.

Our Minister who had shown great interest was very supportive. This time there had been no great problems except perhaps, for an unfounded rumour about the disappearance of Caravaggio's signature on the painting.

As I remarked to my former Minister, this time no one had any adverse criticism to offer! I was so glad to hear his spontaneous response: "Yes, this time things have worked out so much better!"

In a service held at St. John's, the church was packed,

Nave VEGA – P 404

speeches were delivered and the painting – in all its glory, was back in its place in St. John's Oratory.

This time, no one had offered his political acumen, the preying prelate was out of sight, no diplomat had dipped his finger, my 'small man' must have felt even smaller ... and I was feeling so relieved that after the sad experience with the *'St. Jerome'*, *'The Beheading'* had been brought back – 'on a golden platter'.

The *'Beheading of St. John the Baptist'* does have another tale all of its own – and one day will be told in greater detail.

But that is another story ...

"So long Thy power hath blest me
Sure it still will lead me on..."

Portrait of Caravaggio discovered by Mario Buhagiar